ITALIAN CRAFTS

Inspirations From Folk Art

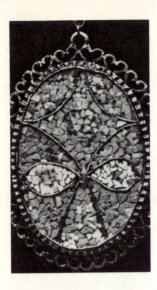

Other books by Janet and Alex D'Amato

American Indian Craft Inspirations
Quillwork, The Craft of Paper Filigree
Gifts to Make for Love or Money
African Crafts for You to Make
Colonial Crafts for You to Make
African Animals Through African Eyes
Handicrafts for Holidays
Cardboard Carpentry

Photographs by Susan Wilson

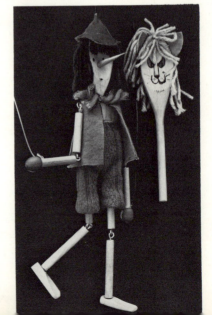

£2-50

ITALIAN CRAFTS

Inspirations From Folk Art

Janet and Alex D'Amato

M. Evans and Company, Inc. /New York, N.Y. 10017

M. Evans and Company titles are distributed in
the United States by the J. B. Lippincott Company,
East Washington Square, Philadelphia, Pa. 19105;
and in Canada by McClelland & Stewart Ltd.,
25 Hollinger Road, Toronto M4B 3G2, Ontario

Library of Congress Cataloging in Publication Data

D'Amato, Janet.
    Italian crafts: inspirations from folk art.

    Includes index.
    1. Handicraft—Italy. 2 Folk art—Italy.
I. D'Amato, Alex, joint author. II. Title.
TT79.D35   745.5'0945   76-30523
ISBN 0-87131-227-1

Design by Alex D'Amato

Manufactured in the United States of America

9 8 7 6 5 4 3 2 1

*This book is dedicated
to my mother, Raffaela Fortuna D'Amato,
who raised us to believe in the Italian proverb:
"Those who use only their hands are
using only half their God given gifts.
Those who use only their minds
are using only half their God given gifts.
But those who use both hands
and minds are using all their God given gifts."
A.D.*

CONTENTS

FOREWORD **9**

1. WITH A BIT OF THREAD **11**
   History: Lace, Quilting, Trapunto, Embroidery, Drawnwork and
   Cutwork, Needle Laces, Other Manipulations of Decorative
   Threads, Bobbin Lace, Folk Dress
   Projects: Embroidered Apron . . . 18, Renaissance Jewel Box
   . . . 21, Florentine Trapunto . . . 25, Tambour . . . 28, Punto in
   Aria . . . 33, Macro-Lace . . . 39

2. MOSAICS **49**
   History: Tesserae, Religious Mosaics, Miniatures, Folk Art,
   Mosaic Methods
   Projects: Midden Mosaics . . . 54, Potshard Pendants . . . 58,
   Mini-Mosaics . . . 59

3. LEATHER **62**
   History: Leather Guilds, Folk Craft, Leather Techniques
   Projects: Leather Bank . . . 64, Encased Bottles . . . 69, Petite
   Patch Pouch . . . 71

4. WOOD AND STRAW **76**
   History: Carving, Intarsia, Marquetry, Parquetry, Straw Mar-
   quetry
   Projects: Chip carving . . . 80, Overlay Bird Bookends . . . 85,
   Inlaid Veneers . . . 88, Balsa Core Jewelry . . . 91, Straw Mar-
   quetry Box . . . 96, Straw Work Plaque . . . 99

5. PAPER **101**
   History: Books and Printing, Art Povero, Religious Cards, Paper
   Filigree and Greeting Cards
   Projects: Quick Trick Art Povero . . . 105, Card Creations . . .
   108, Paper Filigree . . . 111

6. COMBINED MATERIALS: TOYS AND CELEBRATIONS 115
   History: Puppetry in Italy, Holidays and Occasions, Presepio
   Projects: Pinocchio Puppet . . . 122, Presepio: The Setting . . .
   129, Presepio Figurines . . . 134, Ornaments: In Review . . .
   139

7. GENERAL INFORMATION 148
   Materials . . . 148, Basic Tools . . . 148, Stitchery . . . 150,
   Wood . . . 151, Paints, Glues, Finishes . . . 152, Jewelry Find-
   ings . . . 152, To Enlarge Patterns . . . 154, Craft Materials
   Suppliers . . . 155, Bibliography . . . 156

INDEX 158

FOREWORD

The great art of Italy is well known. From the master craftsmen of the Ravenna mosaics to Giotto to the famous artists of the Renaissance—no other country can claim so many great artists. But what of the folk artists? Little has been written or recorded of their creations, probably because there is such a vast store of fine art to explore. Italian museums and churches are filled with huge accumulations. Doubtless any artistic talent would have been appreciated and developed in a country so in love with art. An artisan who carved elaborate biblical scenes on leather wall panels may have learned his skill making leather bottles or sandals, perfecting his craft as he decorated ordinary objects with leather carving.

It is often difficult to distinguish between the professional craftsman and the folk artisan. As a peasant craftsman became more skilled, he may have been able to sell his craft or take on apprentices, being expert enough to teach his craft.

Most art finds its roots in folk art. Italy has one of the oldest continuous civilizations, and, throughout the centuries, crafts were always present. For every great artist, there were thousands of lesser known craftsmen and countless unknown but skilled folk artists.

Artisans of Etruscan and Roman times made various crafts, many of which could be considered folk art. Craft guilds were well established by the Middle Ages. It took years of apprenticeship to learn crafts such as woodcarving, leatherwork, mosaics, glasswork. Rigid tests had to be met before a craftsman could qualify for a guild.

During the Renaissance, arts and crafts of all types flourished. The various city-states of Italy competed for supremacy in the arts. The ruling families of each city-state encouraged and supported the arts and crafts on all levels.

For centuries the Catholic Church has had a powerful influence in Italy and consequently on Italian crafts. A small handmade shrine or devotional picture may have been the only decoration in a poor home. During the Renaissance, the Church was the largest landowner and commissioned the greatest artists and craftsmen. Many crafts were produced by friars and nuns. Girls often learned their needlework from the nuns in the convent.

True folk art was made by and for the family, and much time and care were lavished on these creations. Toys were homemade; a cradle would be carved with loving care for a new child. Household items were embellished to give to a new bride. A farmer's wife might spend all her free time embroidering an apron to wear for a special occasion or a christening gown for a gift. Since these crafts were enjoyed by the family alone, few were saved. They were not considered fine art, and so they did not find their way into museums. Thus, little is known of early folk crafts.

Although folk art has been an expression of man's creative efforts from earliest history, examples are usually shown only from the eighteenth and nineteenth centuries. But folk crafts did not start then, nor did folk art end with the Industrial Revolution. Since folk designs were usually handed down to succeeding generations, what we now call folk art was generally derived from earlier traditions. Each province had indigenous designs and types of crafts.

Today, a disenchantment with machine-made products has resulted in folk art becoming more valued and appreciated. The strong color and design, the intimate detail and artistic values of folk art, are now being recognized, and attempts are being made to preserve this art form.

Each of the following chapters discusses a type of craft for which Italy is particularly noted. Afterward, specific instructions are given to make projects that were inspired by the Italian craft. The history of the craft is interesting just to read; but at the same time we hope it encourages you to find a project you'd like to work on.

Most of the projects have been simplified, using easily obtainable materials and few tools. Descriptions of materials and tools are in Chapter 7. It would be helpful to read these notations before starting any projects. Also listed are sources of suppliers for special craft materials.

These projects are designed to encourage experimenting with new craft techniques, based on traditional crafts. By learning a little about many crafts, you will surely find one that most intrigues you. Then, with the addition of your own creative ideas, it may become your specialty.

Should you wish to know more about the classic methods of a particular craft and want to do more complex projects, you can consult the bibliography. Each book listed devotes an entire volume to one craft, to help you learn all facets of it.

Let's get acquainted with the rich heritage of *l'artigianato Italiano* (Italian crafts).

1

WITH A BIT OF THREAD

Even before recorded history, fibers were spun into strands or threads, which in one way or another were converted into fabrics. Ancient art shows that these antique fabrics were often ornamented. Techniques of sewing, embroidery, netting, quilting, and many others have been refined and elaborated through the centuries.

Wool and flax were the most common threads used up until the last century. Flax could be coarsely spun or, for delicate laces, made as fine as a spider web. Not much cotton was used until the nineteenth century.

Bronze thimbles, scissors, and needles have been found in Roman and Pompeian ruins. Up until the machine age, everyone knew how to sew, and children were taught how to do it at an early age.

Mythical animals and birds appear in this detail of an antique Italian tapestry.

This needlelace pattern is from a Renaissance book by the Venetian designer, Vinciolo.

Lace:

In Italy, by 1500, lace was in great demand. The nobles and wealthy used it lavishly as current fashions decreed. The Church also commissioned large quantities of the finest laces. This extensive use of lace affected the history of the times. Venetian lacemakers were sent to France to teach the art. Skilled laceworkers were sometimes kidnapped into other countries. By the sixteenth century, lace was also being made of gold and silver threads. The poor may have resented the gaudy show of wealth.

As early as 1514, laws were passed in attempts to control the extravagant display of lace. No one under twenty-five could wear lace, and the use of gold and silver threads were curtailed. At one time, Milan prohibited the import of laces, while other areas put taxes on lace.

In the late eighteenth century, lace machines were invented. The early machines made a net to which designs were applied by hand. Gradually other machines were patented (mostly in England) to make all types of lace. By 1870, most lace was machine made.

Quilting, Trapunto:

Two pieces of fabric sewn together with some sort of padding between is an ancient technique for adding warmth or strength. By the thirteenth century, such quilting was used under armor for comfort and protection.

Originally the stitching just held the stuffing in place. The Latin word *culcita* or *culcitra* means "a sack filled." Gradually the sewing together became more decorative and was used for bedding as well as armor and clothing.

One of the oldest quilts still in existence is a bedcovering from Sicily from the fourteenth century. Detailed scenes illustrating legends are stitched with brown threads on the linen quilt.

Trapunto, often called "Italian quilting," consists of sewing two layers together with only certain planned areas to be stuffed. A cord or stuffing is inserted into these areas from behind. Trapunto does not add warmth, as does the quilting on bedcoverings, but gives only a decorative effect. Florentine trapunto has a transparent top with colored cords between the layers.

Embroidery:

This is a basic method of adding design by sewing colored threads onto a surface. Often, embroidery samplers were made by young girls so that they could learn the stitches and insure that the family design would be remembered and passed on.

Drawnwork and Cutwork:

As embroidery became more and more complex, layers and layers of stitches often became too heavy. Sometime around 1500, techniques developed for either cutting away some of the fabric or pulling out certain threads behind the embroidery to make the finished piece lighter. Cutwork and drawnwork (*punto tirato*), became important needlework methods. Since removing threads was tedious, a special weave fabric (*buratto*) was made, with space between threads to be filled with needlework.

In cutwork, threads were sewn across an area of fabric; then these threads were covered with buttonhole stitching to make designs. Finally, the fabric behind was cut away. *Punto tagliato* eventually developed into the famous needle laces of Italy.

This sixteenth century valance (''Wedding Train'') from Sicily, is a classic example of Buratto.

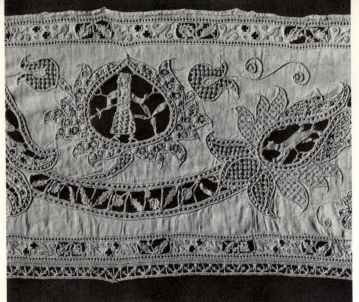

An example of Italian cutwork on linen, from the early seventeenth century; vines are worked in punto reale *and the figures in the open areas (cut work) are examples of* punto in aria. *Edge is needle lace* (reticello).

Needle Laces:

Reticella lace was worked over a pattern basted between two edges of fabric. Early examples of this lace were geometric; later, all sorts of motifs, even human figures and animals, were stitched into the design.

Punto in aria literally means "to embroider in air." The threads were no longer worked into a fabric. Buttonhole-type stitches were worked onto a framework or mesh of threads attached to a pattern.

This method of lace-making, known as needle lace, was used extensively in churches and for household items and clothing of the sixteenth and seventeenth centuries, including the large standing "Medici collar" with lace cuffs and flounces. Lace continued to be widely used on both men's and women's clothing throughout the eighteenth century. Though less extravagant, some needle lace was still in fashion well into the nineteenth century.

Other Manipulations of Decorative Threads:

Combining threads to create effects can take many forms. Knitting on spools or needles was done as far back as the Middle Ages. This method of creating a garment, hat, or stocking was usually done by men.

Manipulating a thread with a hook was originally done through a fabric stretched on a frame called a *tambour*. It's believed this came to Europe from the Near East. The thread, held in back, was hooked up onto the front, creating surface designs. By the end of the eighteenth century, tambouring was done "in aria," that is, without the fabric. Today we know it as crocheting.

Netting, also very ancient, was made with a shuttle, for practical uses, especially by fishermen. Almost every home had a shuttle; even noble ladies had large shuttles to make the nets needed in the fields for a hunter to carry his catch. Of course, a noble lady probably also had a fine shuttle for making delicate net lace.

Knotting (macrame) was another method used to make nets or decorative edgings. These edgings were good for ornamentations for bed hangings, but the knots tended to be bulky and uncomfortable for clothing. The long ends necessary to make a large piece were kept from tangling by winding ends around a stick or bone. This could have been the origin of bobbin lace.

Bobbin Lace:

Although bobbins have been found in Roman ruins, no lace has survived from ancient Rome. So there is no evidence that bobbin lace was made before the fifteenth century. By the sixteenth century, Milan, Florence, Genoa, and Venice had become centers for this type of lace.

Bobbin lace, formed by twisting or braiding manipulation (rather than by knotting), was worked on a pattern attached to a special pillow. Pins

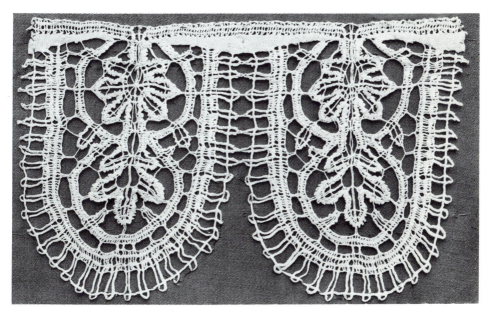

An example of seventeenth century bobbin lace; other designs were more complex, requiring hundreds of bobbins.

An Italian peasant woman is working bobbin lace on a pillow.

stuck into the pattern held each crossing of the thread, and thus the design was created. Each thread was weighted by a bobbin which also held extra lengths of thread. As some threads were so thin they could hardly be seen, bobbins were needed to handle them.

Each family of laceworkers had one design which they handed down from generation to generation. It was never altered; creativity was not part of the craft then. To earn extra money, many a farmer's wife had a "pillow" on which lace was always in progress. It could take as long as a year to make a yard of detailed bobbin lace.

By the age of four, children started learning the bobbin lace technique with a few bobbins. By the age of sixteen, a girl was usually skilled enough to make lace designs requiring hundreds of bobbins.

Bobbin lace, difficult and tedious to produce, was usually made by the peasants. When noble ladies made lace, it was generally some type of needle lace.

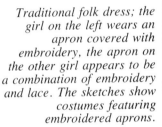

Traditional folk dress; the girl on the left wears an apron covered with embroidery, the apron on the other girl appears to be a combination of embroidery and lace. The sketches show costumes featuring embroidered aprons.

Folk Dress:

Some of the finest examples of folk crafts can be seen on peasant costumes. Years of work could go into the creation of clothing to be worn for festivals or given for a special occasion. Each family and each area had an individual style.

Origins of the style probably went back to a time when it was the current fashion of the day. Frequently peasant costumes for women had a large-sleeved blouse with a tight bodice, a full skirt, and a long colorful apron which was often lavishly embroidered. Many aprons had lace trims. But there was no one style that could be called Italian; each province had its own distinct style. The sketches here show a few styles picked at random.

In the late nineteenth century, after Italy was unified, folk costumes were seen less frequently. As machine-made laces and decorations became available, fewer were handmade by the new generations.

Embroidered Apron

A combination of embroidery, rick-rack, and decorative tapes creates the designs on this ankle length apron.

Folk costume handwork can be revived as inspiration for contemporary clothes. This colorful apron could be made of cotton and used with casual clothes (pants) or it could be made of a silk-type fabric and worn with a long skirt for more festive occasions.

MATERIALS

1 yard dark material, 45″ wide; 2¼ yards decorative embroidered tape or ribbon, 1½-1¾″ wide (or 3 pieces in different designs, 18″, 28″, and 31″); 2 packages baby rick-rack; 2 yards decorative narrow tape, ¼″ or ½″ wide (or 1 each of different designs).

Needle, thimble, thread to match fabric; dressmaker transfer paper and wheel (from sewing store); 7″ embroidery hoop; large-eyed embroidery needle; embroidery floss (at least 3 or 4 colors, 2 skeins of the dominant color).

Choose a dark fabric (not a stretch type) such as black, dark blue, or dark green. Select a colorful embroidered tape or ribbon; its background should harmonize with or match the fabric. This selection is important for the appearance of the finished apron. A two-color embroidered tape is usually less expensive than three or four colors. You can add more colors in the design yourself, if you like. For instance (Fig. 1), add spots of yellow and green to a band of machine embroidery done only in blue and white on black.

The selection of the wide tape should determine the general color scheme. Make it something lively such as blue, white, and red with touches of green and yellow. Buy rick-rack, narrower tapes, and embroidery floss to complete the color scheme.

For the apron, make a paper pattern using old newspapers taped together (or use an old sheet). Draw sizes shown (Fig. 2), and adjust to suit your height and waist. Cut paper pattern (Fig. 3) and try on. Top part folds

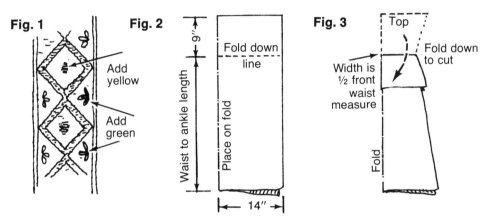

over a belt and will hang in front (Fig. 4). Adjust to fit your waistline. It should fit fairly smoothly from side seam to other side without much gathering. Mark length desired, allowing for 1½″ hem. When dimensions have been determined, pin the paper pattern to the fabric, and cut out.

Turn 1½″ under at bottom and hem (Fig. 5). Fold top edge under 1¼″, making sure fold is in reverse direction (for when it folds over belt).

Make a narrow rolled hem up the side, tapering off at fold (X on Fig. 5). Turn fabric over and roll hem on reverse side for top layer. Repeat, hemming up the other side.

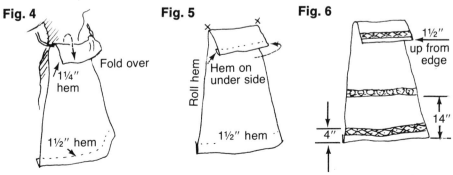

Lay apron flat; lay on the tapes, edgings, and rick-rack to plan arrangement. Space somewhat as shown (Fig. 6), adjusting to width of braid and tapes you have. Allow about ¾″ extra on each side; cut off and pin in place. Sew bands to apron with invisible stitches (Fig. 7). At each side fold tapes around to back and sew, keeping as flat as possible.

Basic embroidery stitches are diagrammed in Chapter 7 under "Stitchery." If you have never done embroidery before, practice each stitch on scrap fabric. Stretch the fabric on the embroidery hoop and stitch a row or two until you are familiar with the stitches.

Fig. 7

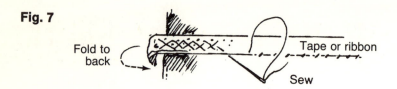

Fold to back

Tape or ribbon

Sew

On paper, enlarge the design in figure 8; trace the other half. Transfer to apron, just above the bottom row of tapes, using white or yellow dressmaker carbon transfer paper and wheel. On folded-over top of apron, draw a row of loops just above decorative tape (Fig. 9). The solid zigzag lines in the pattern indicate placement of baby rick-rack. Sew in position.

Fig. 8

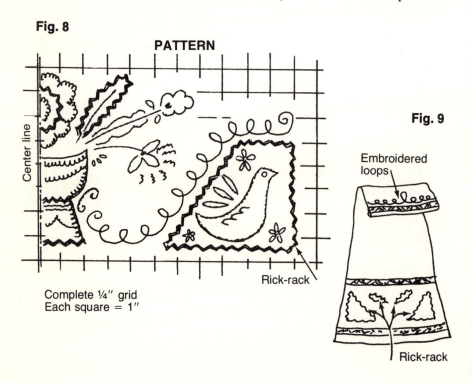

PATTERN

Center line

Fig. 9

Embroidered loops

Rick-rack

Complete ¼″ grid
Each square = 1″

Rick-rack

Stretch apron fabric on hoop and embroider a section at a time, using six-strand embroidery floss. Arrange colors to make attractive designs, such as a bluebird with red wings. With a satin stitch you can add color to the machine-embroidered tapes (See Fig. 1). Add any other motifs that might appeal to you. Press edges if needed. Wear by slipping over a sash or belt (see Fig. 4).

Machine-embroidered tapes were used to create effects more quickly. But if you are very ambitious, the entire apron can be hand embroidered—to become a real heirloom treasure.

Renaissance Jewel Box

A piece of discarded bulky costume jewelry forms the front lift on this box, which is covered with pale blue brocade and edged in gold.

A piece of elegant fabric and a length of braid can transform an old box into a Renaissance-looking treasure.

MATERIALS

Wooden box (old or new) at least 6″ long; fabric large enough to cover box (brocade or other elegant texture); lighter weight fabric (for lining); gold braid; felt to cover base of box.

Several pieces of lightweight cardboard (cereal box or pad back); 4 round shank buttons; serrated knife; paper; masking tape; paint (to match lining fabric); brush; rubber bands; clip clothespins; Sobo glue.

For converting a flat top into a rounded-top box: rigid packing foam about 1″ thick or Styrofoam® brand plastic foam* the size of top of box (from craft store); latch (from craft store) or piece of costume jewelry (optional).

*Trademark of the Dow Chemical Company

Remove top of box, keeping screws and hinges until needed. First make card pieces for the lining of the box. Measure and cut a separate piece of card (Fig. 1) for each inside surface (10 units). Make each piece ¼″ smaller than the inside measurement of box. Cut lining fabric at least ⅛″ larger than card, on each side (Fig. 2). Trim out corners. Add glue to edge of card back as shown (Fig. 3). Do not get any glue on front; be sure to keep fabric clean. Fold fabric around, stretch slightly, and press down. Fabric in front should be taut, but not so tight that card buckles. Trim away any overlap at back. Hold with clothespins or weights until dry. Continue until all pieces of card are covered.

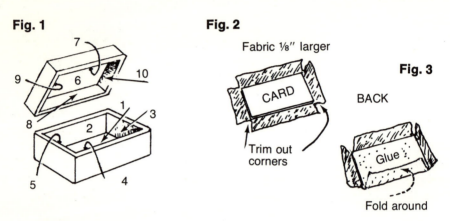

Fig. 1

Fig. 2

Fabric ⅛″ larger

CARD

Trim out corners

Fig. 3

BACK

Glue

Fold around

Place fabric-covered card in bottom inside of box. Place the four fabric-covered cards around sides. Check that all fit neatly. If they are too large (depending on bulkiness of fabric used), some pieces may need to be trimmed. Remove, pull fabric back along one edge, trim card slightly. Reglue the fabric around trimmed edge and replace in box again, to check fit. Repeat for inside top of box. Make sure none of the fabric-covered cards protrudes over edges to prevent box from closing. Trim as before, if necessary. When all pieces fit properly, remove them and set them aside.

A flat top box can be transformed into a round top, or you may be fortunate enough to find a box with a curved top. To convert a flat top, use rigid foam (e.g., Styrofoam). Mark area of box top. With a serrated knife, cut shape, then whittle front and back edges of piece to form a curved surface (Fig. 4). Use a scrap of foam like sandpaper to rub against and smooth the surface. Place on top of box to check shape.

Measure width of box. Take a piece of the lightweight card and cut to measured width. Wrap and curve it around the cut foam piece (Fig. 5); fold under about 1″, trim off. Spread glue over entire undersurface of the card, wrap around shape, and hold with rubber bands until glue is dry. Make sure it still fits top of box.

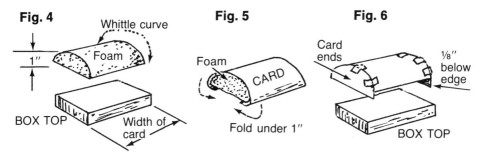

On another piece of card, trace around each end of the piece where foam shows. Add about ⅛″ on straight edge. Cut two pieces, and glue to ends (Fig. 6). Hold edges together with masking tape. (Tape can be left on for extra sturdiness, since fabric will cover it.) Glue cardboard-covered unit to top of box ⅛″ overlapping ends of box top.

Paint inside top edge of box and cover (Fig. 7); these are the only areas that will show. Now it is ready for the fabric.

The quality of the fabric you choose is important. Use upholstery scraps or fabric sample, sturdy but not too bulky. Interesting remnants can sometimes be found at bazaars and garage sales. If you can't find a suitable piece, use wide decorative ribbon, preferably the width of the base of the box. Plan to attach decorative braid to hide each joining (Fig. 8).

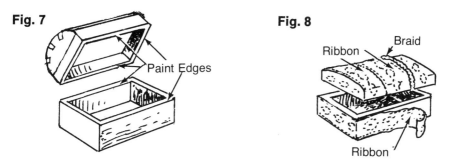

Before cutting fabric, make paper patterns of ends, front, back, over top, and side of top. Arrange patterns making best possible use of the design on the fabric. Cut out, making pieces slightly larger than pattern. Spread glue on one surface of the box at a time, in an even coat, not too thick. Stick on fabric piece and pull taut. Press down and trim fabric even with box edge. Keep smoothing as glue dries to make sure fabric has adhered properly.

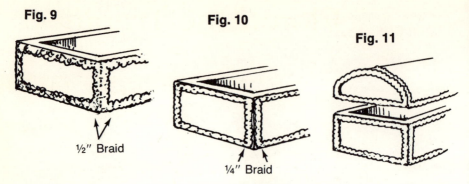

Fig. 9

Fig. 10

Fig. 11

½" Braid

¼" Braid

All the raw edges will be hidden by gold braid (available in craft stores and many sewing and variety stores). A braid about ½" wide can be folded around corners (Fig. 9), or use narrower braid and place on each side of corners (Fig. 10). Cover all edges (Fig. 11). Before adding braid at back, reattach the hinges, placing them over the fabric but under the braid.

Add gold braid trim to top as desired for more elegance. Or, if you pieced the fabric from small scraps, add the braid where pieces meet (Fig. 12).

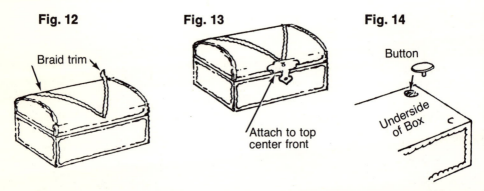

Fig. 12

Braid trim

Fig. 13

Attach to top center front

Fig. 14

Button

Underside of Box

To replace lining, add dabs of glue to inside bottom and sides of box. Fit in the lining pieces and press in place. Glue lining pieces in box top also.

A handle or ornate lift is not necessary but adds to the appearance as well as keeping the fabric clean as box is used. Use a decorative clasp or a discarded piece of costume jewelry. Attach with tiny screws or glue in place (Fig. 13).

Cover the bottom of the box with felt or fabric. For feet, use the shank buttons or screw-in feet made for boxes (from craft stores). If using buttons, cut a hole in the felt (Fig. 14) and whittle a small hole in the box to accommodate the shank. When it fits easily, add glue and push it in place. The box is now complete, a cache for your own treasures or an elegant gift.

Florentine Trapunto

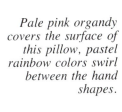

Pale pink organdy covers the surface of this pillow, pastel rainbow colors swirl between the hand shapes.

It is difficult to adequately photograph the subtle color effects created with Florentine trapunto. Only by seeing and touching it can it be appreciated. Colored yarns are threaded through stitched channels of translucent color, subtly altering their hues and dimension. Make a pillow and see the effect for yourself.

MATERIALS

½ yd. pastel-colored organdy (such as pink or pale blue); ½ yd. cotton fabric for backing (in a compatible color); yarns of various colors; sewing thread to match organdy; stuffing.

    Dressmaker carbon tracing paper and wheel (from sewing store); blunt, large-eyed yarn needle; embroidery floss and needle (optional).

The design for the pillow shown (I call it ''Rainbow Reaching'') can be drawn freehand to make any size pillow. Overall dimensions will be at least 1″ less after working the design, so allow for this. For a 14″ pillow, figure 15″ plus 1″ on each side for seaming. Cut a 17″ square of cotton fabric and 17″ square of organdy.

Fig. 1

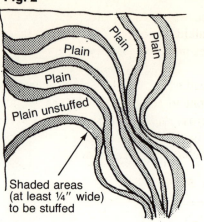

Fig. 2

Plain

Plain

Plain

Plain

Plain unstuffed

) Shaded areas
(at least ¼″ wide)
to be stuffed

On 17″ area on paper, plan the design. Trace around your hand on corners as shown (Fig. 1), making fat fingers (they skinny up when stuffed). Draw the rainbow swirl lines between to the two opposite corners. Keep in mind that you will be pulling yarn between these lines. Space between lines can vary but should not be less than ¼″. Draw lines in pairs and plan open unstuffed areas (Fig. 2).

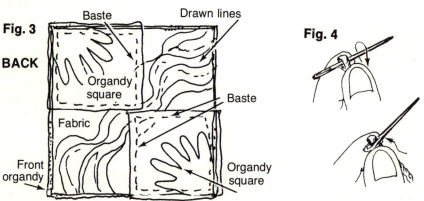

Fig. 3

BACK

Baste

Drawn lines

Organdy
square

Baste

Fabric

Front
organdy

Organdy
square

Fig. 4

When design is drawn, transfer to back of cotton fabric using the tracing wheel and dressmaker's transfer paper.

Cut a square of organdy to cover each drawn hand area (Fig. 3); baste over transferred design. This is the back of the work. Turn over, place the 17″ organdy square over front, and baste around outside edges (about 15″ square).

Turn over again and work from the back. Machine-stitch through all layers, along all the drawn lines, including hand outlines.

The colored yarn used to fill the stitched channels will show through the organdy on the front. Try various yarns under some scraps of organdy to see which colors are most effective. Any type of yarn can be used, the bulkier the better. Gro-Point yarns, gift wrap ties (from card shops), or hair ties are good, as they fill the design more rapidly.

Thread large-eyed needle with yarn by flattening the yarn around the needle (Fig. 4), then push flattened edge through the eye. Working from the front to see effects achieved, slide yarn through a stitched channel. Pull across channel and out at other edge. Cut off, leaving about ½" beyond edge (Fig. 5). If channel widens, add more yarn of same color to fill it. Use yarn double on wide channels.

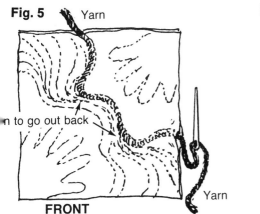

Fig. 5 Yarn

n to go out back

FRONT

Yarn

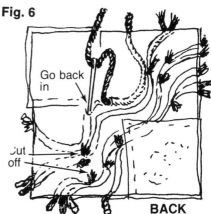

Fig. 6

Go back in

Cut off

BACK

If the channel narrows somewhere in the middle, run yarn as far as it will go. Then poke the needle out through cotton fabric in the back (Fig. 6). Clip yarn, leaving about ½" sticking out. If a turn is too sudden, go out back and come in again. If necessary to get yarn out, clip cotton fabric a bit in the back. Make sure organdy in front is not damaged in any way. There will be many exits of yarn in the back as you work (Fig. 6). Fill all planned areas with rainbow colors, leaving some background fabric showing (see Fig. 2).

The hands are regular trapunto (that is, stuffed). As stuffing would be unattractive showing through on front, stuffing will go behind the cotton background fabric. Turn piece over to *back*. In the organdy pieces on the

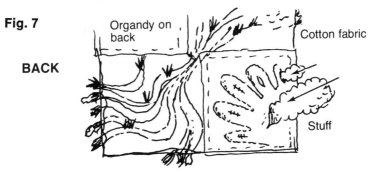

Fig. 7

Organdy on back

Cotton fabric

BACK

Stuff

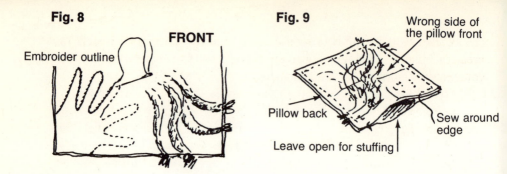

Fig. 8

Embroider outline

FRONT

Fig. 9

Wrong side of the pillow front

Pillow back

Sew around edge

Leave open for stuffing

back of the work, behind hands, cut small slits. (Do not cut any organdy on the front.) Poke fluffs of stuffing up into each finger shape and lightly pad hand area (Fig. 7). Sew these slits closed if necessary. Turn over. If desired, to show up contour of hands, embroider a colored outline (Fig. 8) around each hand on front (see Chapter 7, Stitchery).

To finish pillow, cut a piece of cotton fabric for back to match present size of front. Place right sides together. Baste, making it as square as possible (Fig. 9). Sew around three sides and part of fourth. Turn right side out, fill firmly with stuffing, and sew remaining edge closed.

Try this interesting effect for clothing, possibly a vest or skirt.

Tambour

Folk Art designs were the inspiration for the tambour piece that enhances the tote bag. The small sun, still in progress on the embroidery hoop, may become a hot mat or pot holder.

Centuries ago, tambour was usually done on linen with fine threads creating traceries of pattern over the fabric. Today you can make a more contemporary look with yarn and burlap using the same technique.

MATERIALS

Burlap; knitting yarn (in colors desired); crochet hook (proper size for yarn used—I used an E with regular knitting worsted); embroidery hoop; waterproof felt marker.

First the basic method will be described. Try it on a scrap of burlap and then decide what you'd like to make. Some suggestions will follow. What you make will determine the size of burlap and colors of yarn you need, four-ply knitting yarn is good, but any similar yarn could be used.

To practice, cut a piece of burlap to fit embroidery hoop and stretch it onto hoop. One hand will stay below hoop to guide the yarn as it comes off the ball. The other hand manipulates the crochet hook above the hoop. Push

Fig. 1

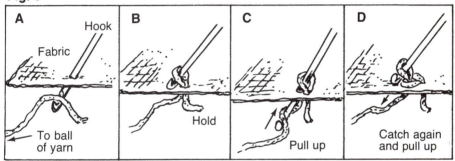

the hook down through the burlap and catch yarn in hook, using other hand to place it in hook. Hook yarn about 2″ from starting end (Fig. 1A). Pull yarn loop up through burlap, creating a loop over the hook (Fig. 1B). Go down into the burlap, next hole over, and again catch yarn below. Pull up and through the loop already over the hook. Now there is a new loop on the hook (Fig. 1C). Push down through the burlap again (Fig. 1D), hook, and repeat. Once you get the simple rhythm of it—down through, hook, pull up through loop on hook, and repeat—it is a simple process repeated throughout the design. Those who crochet will find it familiar. The entire surface will be filled with the looped design created (Fig. 2), row upon row. Don't pull too tight, yarn loops should lay flat on surface.

Fig. 2

Fig. 3

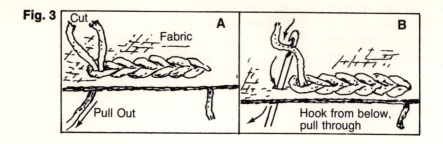

Fig. 4

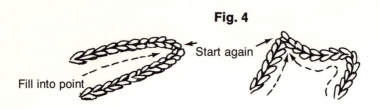

When you come to the end of a design or color area, pull the last loop up about 1½″ and cut at top (Fig. 3A). With hand below hoop, pull on yarn to remove half of the loop. Reach under hoop with the crochet hook, push up from back, and pull through the remaining end (Fig. 3B). When filling in a point of the deign or making sharp turns it's often easier to cut off and start again (Fig. 4). If you need to add a bit of another color, the first color can be left hanging, work in with new color, then go back and work first color.

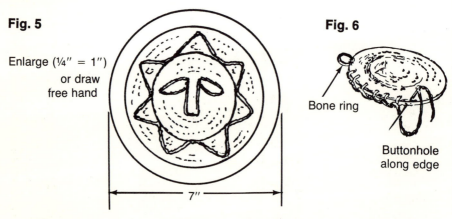

Fig. 5 is a pattern for a round piece than can be made on a 7″-diameter embroidery hoop. Cut burlap about 2″ larger. Draw the design on burlap with waterproof felt markers. Stretch burlap on the hoop and work the design in bright colors, yellows and pink background. Or use any colors left from other yarn projects. Outline edges with black or dark brown. The rows of loops made, about ⅛" wide, make design, color, and texture as they fill the surface. Cover surface completely so no burlap shows. Remove from hoop and press, if necessary.

You probably have some ideas about what to do with this circle. Cut burlap edges about 1" away from work. Turn edges under so no burlap shows. You can sew this circle to the back of a jacket or a bag. You can glue it on top of a trinket box. It can also be used to make a pot holder. For thickness, cut a 7" circle of terry cloth or felt. Cut a circle of felt for back. Baste the three pieces together. Blanket-stitch around (see Chapter 7, Stitchery), to finish edges. Sew on a bone ring (Fig. 6) for hanging.

Now that the technique is familiar, you can try something larger.

MATERIALS

15" x 16" piece of burlap; brightly colored yarns; crochet hook; embroidery hoop; waterproof felt markers; ½ yd. of sturdy fabric (for tote); matching thread.

The pattern (Fig. 1) was derived from an Italian rug design of the seventeenth century. Such motifs were probably mythological, handed

Fig. 1

PATTERN

Draw grid of ¼" squares, enlarge to 1" squares.

Overall size
12" x 14"

See photo, page 28

down and stylized. Enlarge pattern (see Chapter 7 for how to enlarge). Draw on burlap. Use brightly colored yarns for a folk look—try black outlines with red, blue, orange, and green. The stag could be in white. Tambour the black outlines first; then fill in colors until surface is completely covered.

As this square is larger, it will be necessary to move it on the embroidery hoop as work progresses (unless you have a very large hoop). When considerable yarn has been worked on the fabric, it becomes too thick to place in the hoop. The last fill-in will have to be done without any hoop. The design may alter somewhat from pattern as it depends on where rows of tambour are placed. This helps give the piece a folk look.

For a wall decoration, trim edges to within 1″ of the design, fold back, and sew to a felt panel. Or sew tambour piece to a canvas tote bag. If you can't find a bag the proper size, you can make one of canvas or denim or other sturdy material. Cut a piece of fabric as shown (Fig. 2). Fold under edges of tambour panel so no burlap shows, and sew in place on fabric. Sew up sides of bag. Hem top. Handles can be made of leftover fabric (Fig. 3) or rope. Fold and stitch length for strength. Sew in position indicated in Fig. 2.

Now that you know basic tambour, you can experiment with designs of your choice. Try fine threads on linen, or colored threads loosely rambling across a curtain. When you use attractive fabric for backing you need not fill it solid with design. Use tambour to add initials to a fabric (Fig. 4).

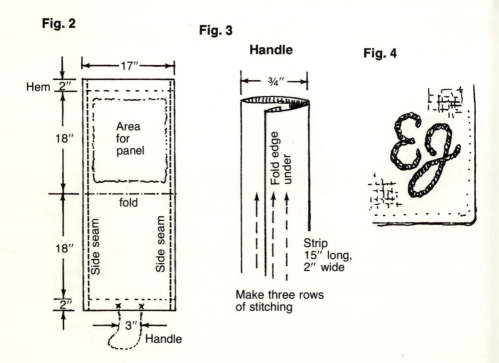

Fig. 2

Fig. 3

Handle

Fig. 4

17″

Hem 2″

Area for panel

18″

fold

Side seam

Side seam

18″

2″

3″

Handle

¾″

Fold edge under

Strip 15″ long, 2″ wide

Make three rows of stitching

Punto in Aria

A basic practice square was worked on the end of a woolen scarf, the fabric cut from behind. Then the needle lace technique was used to create a decorative "Seed Tree" on a small mirror.

Reticella, cutwork, needle lace—each begins with the same basic threads across a square. Then the threads are embroidered over, *Punto tagliato*. With thin threads, it's a highly skilled craft that takes years to perfect, but it's interesting to learn its basic structure by working on a larger scale, as in the sampler below. Then contemporary adaptations can be made.

MATERIALS
Fabric (such as tightly woven cotton or wool); embroidery floss or Persian yarn; needle; embroidery hoop.

Work a basic needle lace square on fabric. The finished piece could be used as a pocket, appliqued to a purse flap or worked at end of a long piece of fabric to be used for a scarf or sash. If using wool, work design with yarn; on other fabrics, use crochet cotton or embroidery floss. Choose a needle with large enough eye to accommodate thread chosen. Three basic stitches are used. The running stitch (Fig. 1) goes into the fabric. Overcast (Fig. 2), and buttonhole stitches (Fig. 3) are worked over a thread framework.

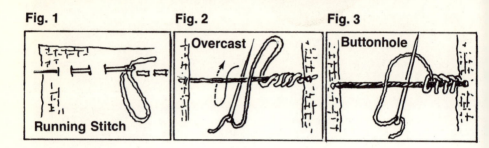

Fig. 1 Running Stitch   **Fig. 2** Overcast   **Fig. 3** Buttonhole

Draw a 2″ square on the fabric. Lay a framework of threads across the square following steps shown in Fig. 4. Needle goes into fabric only around outside drawn square, using running stitches from corner to corner. Area inside square will be cut away when stitching is completed. Start at A, go to corner across square, catching thread in corner. Overcast back along diagonal thread. Go to next corner, make other diagonal, overcast back. With running stitch, go back to A.

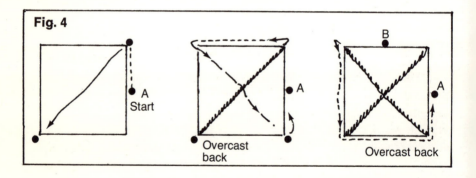

Then make corner diagonals: A, B, C, D. Catch in fabric at B and continue around (Fig. 5) back to A. Now make buttonhole stitches over threads A, B, C, D and back to A. Keep stitches even and tight together; don't allow them to twist. When crossing overcast diagonal, catch it in (Fig. 6). Add another row of corner diagonals, E to L, (Fig. 7) and buttonhole-stitch over these.

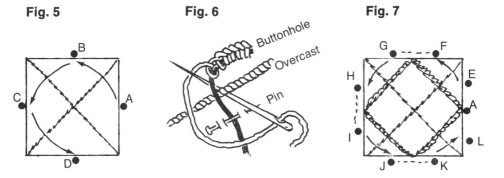

Fig. 5   Fig. 6   Fig. 7

Make a center circle by going up from A, and pin (Fig. 8). Go to point N, pin, and go down to B, overcast back up to N, over to point O, down into fabric at C; overcast back up and continue around in this manner back to pinned point above A. Now buttonhole around this the center area, catching in the diagonals. When around, work another row by making stitches into top of each buttonhole stitch. Try to keep a circular shape as you work (Fig. 9). When complete, overcast back down to A. If necessary to start new threads, make a few running stitches along edge or run a new thread through middle of buttonhole stitches. Do not make knots.

After completing, carefully cut fabric square away next to running stitches, making an open area behind the embroidered work. Fold raw edges back and buttonhole-stitch around square (Fig. 10).

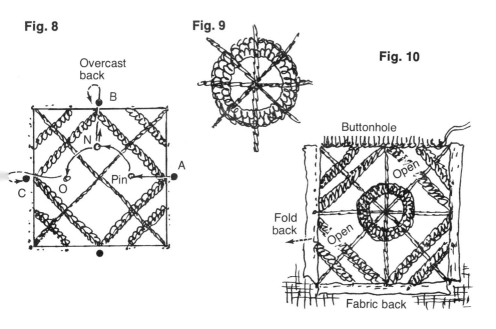

Fig. 8   Fig. 9   Fig. 10

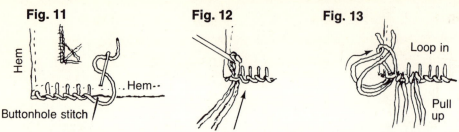

Fig. 11 **Fig. 12** **Fig. 13**

Hem

Buttonhole stitch

..Hem--

Loop in

Pull up

If making a scarf, hem all edges. Buttonhole-stitch along bottom edge (Fig. 11), spacing stitches about ¼" apart, and add a fringe. Pull lengths of yarn through stitches with a crochet hook (Fig. 12), and loop as shown (Fig. 13).

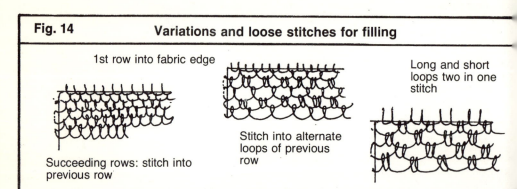

Fig. 14 **Variations and loose stitches for filling**

1st row into fabric edge

Succeeding rows: stitch into previous row

Stitch into alternate loops of previous row

Long and short loops two in one stitch

There are countless variations of the buttonhole stitch (Fig. 14). If you like needleworking, you should explore further. However, the mirror ornament shown, ''The Seed Tree,'' can be made with the basic stitch only.

MATERIALS

Mirror about 5" x 7"; sturdy, heavy cardboard; sturdy fabric and felt (about 9" x 12" each); crochet cotton (Cro-sheen, medium thickness); beads not more than 3/16" diameter.

Large-eyed needle; glue; knife and ruler (to cut card); pins; masking tape; fine needle and thread to match crochet cotton; flat picture hanger or pop-top.

This sort of mirror can usually be purchased in notions departments. Remove and discard the frame, set mirror aside. Usually there is a corrugated card backing; save this. On the heavyweight card, draw an outline of the mirror. Add 1" all around. Cut this frame (Fig. 1).

To cover frame, use a plain sturdy-texture fabric such as cotton or linen. Cut a piece ½" larger all around than frame (Fig. 1). Trim corners.

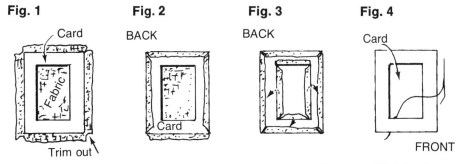

Fig. 1 Card / Fabric / Trim out

Fig. 2 BACK / Card

Fig. 3 BACK

Fig. 4 Card / FRONT

Add glue in back and fold fabric around (Fig. 2), pulling taut. Weight down and allow to dry. Then cut inner area, about ½″ in; slit corners. Add glue and fold in (Fig. 3), creating a fabric-covered frame.

Place corrugated card in opening (or cut a piece to fit). Hold in back with masking tape. Punto in aria will be created in the open area inside the frame (to go over the mirror); see photo. Draw general shape on the corrugated card. Thread needle with crochet cotton and make the thread framework to work on. Come up through fabric at inner edge of frame, leaving thread hanging in back (Fig. 4). Later these ends will be trimmed and glued down. Tape or hold if necessary. First lay framework for tree (Fig. 5). Pin into card at intersections as needed to hold shape. Make fence as shown in Fig. 6, pinning at each point.

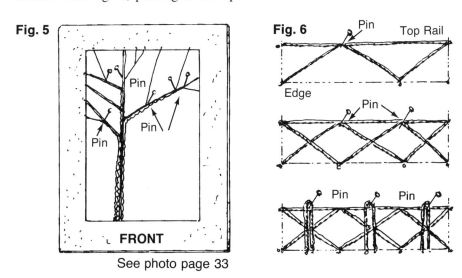

Fig. 5 Pin / Pin / Pin / Pin / **FRONT**

See photo page 33

Fig. 6 Pin / Top Rail / Edge / Pin / Pin / Pin

Buttonhole up tree trunk and out one branch. At end, for twig, overcast instead of buttonhole (Fig. 7). Repeat, working entire tree. Branches should be narrower than limbs; the trunk should be the thickest with at least four rows of stitching.

37

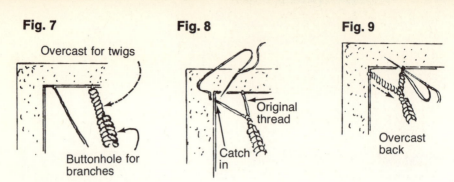

Fig. 7

Overcast for twigs

Buttonhole for branches

Fig. 8

Original thread

Catch in

Fig. 9

Overcast back

To make extra twigs, instead of overcasting on original thread as buttonholing comes near edge, catch in fabric edge about ¼″ away (Fig. 8). Then overcast back, and out again on original thread (Fig. 9).

Always work to edge and catch in fabric with stitches made as invisible as possible. When tree is complete, buttonhole-stitch over fence. Pin and repin as necessary to hold shapes. Make two rows on posts and fence top.

Remove all pins and the piece of card. Place mirror to check effect. Trim any hanging threads. Remove mirror, turn frame over, trim and glue down all loose ends in back, keeping away from edge (Fig. 10).

For "seed" effect, sew beads onto the needlepoint tree. Thread a fine needle with sewing thread to match the crochet cotton. Don't make knot in end; just slide in through buttonhole stitching for about ½″, then come out, go through a bead, back into stitches, and out again into another bead. Make several clusters in appropriate places (see photo). Occasionally sew on two beads by coming out through a larger bead, then through a smaller one, and back through the larger (Fig. 11). Sew back into stitches to hold.

Clean mirror; replace in frame. Tape across corners in back to hold position. Tape a hanger at center top (Fig. 12). Cut a piece of felt slightly smaller than overall frame size. Add glue to frame back, over hanger and to edge of mirror; not on mirror back. Glue felt to back, shaping down around mirror, hiding all threads and raw edges. Punto in aria is used here to make a mirror to look at rather than into.

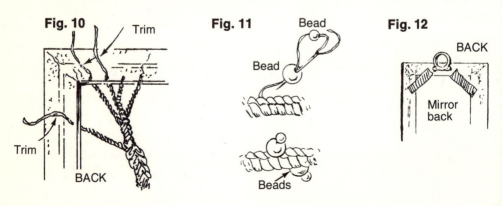

Fig. 10

Trim

Trim

BACK

Fig. 11

Bead

Bead

Beads

Fig. 12

BACK

Mirror back

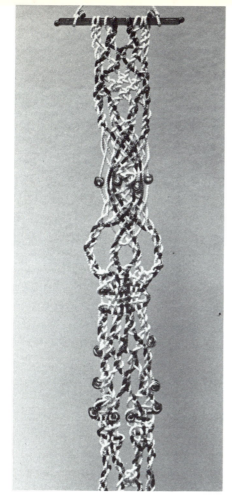

Macro-Lace

Although making lace with fine threads and many bobbins takes skill, even a beginner can make this wall hanging using only eight sets of bobbins and cords rather than threads.

Traditionally, bobbin lace was made with predetermined patterns, using very fine threads. For contemporary looks, cords or yarns can be used to make larger, looser creations. Depending on the inclination of the craftsman, the lace can be a formal or a random design. But first, the basic motions must be mastered. The following sampler will help you do this.

MATERIALS
Cords or yarn; cardboard (for bobbins); 16 metal washers; pins (such as hatpins or macrame "T" pins from craft store); 2 pieces of corrugated cardboard, about 10″ x 12″; masking tape.

Bobbin lace has no knots. It is created by a plaiting process consisting of only two basic motions. All bobbin lace designs are created by a combination of these motions. It is necessary to practice and become very familiar with these basic motions. Then you can create your own designs or master some of the more traditional ones.

To practice, make a sampler of inexpensive easily obtainable material. Get the feel of lacemaking and see how you like it. Then, if you wish to do more specialized projects, it's possible to purchase materials made especially for this craft (see list of suppliers, Chapter 7). Some suppliers also sell booklets with diagrams of basic and complex patterns, bobbins, and other laceworking materials. The bibliography lists some books which give instructions to make all sorts of variations. There is room here for only the basics.

For sampler, use any cord (at least 1/16″ diameter); kitchen string with a hard twist, wrapping cord, or cords sold for macrame. Bobbins can be improvised of cardboard. Cut sixteen pieces of cardboard 1″ x 3″ and shape as shown in Fig. 1. The purpose of the bobbins is twofold: to keep ends in proper sequence and to add weight for proper tension. To get this needed weight, tape a ¾″ metal washer onto the card. Depending on the weight of the cord you are using, you might need a heavier washer or other weight. Straight wood clothespins or 3″ bolts with nuts can be used as bobbins instead. For a working board, tape together two pieces of corrugated cardboard. If desired, cover with a durable fabric.

Cut eight pieces of cord, each one a yard long. Mount the cords on the board by pinning at middle of each cord. Make row at top of the board. Or mount the cords on a stick such as a dowel, skewer stick, or stirrer as shown in Fig. 2. Place pins at each end of stick to attach to board.

Wind end of each cord onto a bobbin. Leave about 6″ hanging from the top. Slip cord through slit to keep it from unwinding (Fig. 3). If using

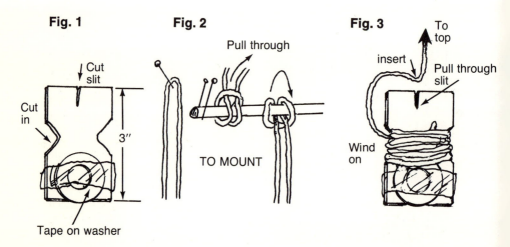

Fig. 1

Cut
slit

Cut
in

3″

Tape on washer

Fig. 2

Pull through

TO MOUNT

Fig. 3

To top

insert

Pull through slit

Wind on

clothespins (or bolt) for bobbins, make a loop knot at top to hold (Fig. 4). Lay bobbins in order (Fig. 5). The board is now ready for you to start learning the basics.

Fig. 4

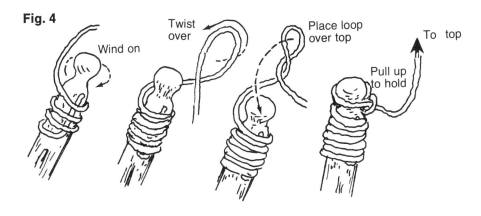

Wind on — Twist over — Place loop over top — To top — Pull up to hold

Always work with two bobbins (a pair) in each hand. Start at left. Take first two bobbins in left hand, next two in right hand; hold them palms up (Fig. 6).

The first basic motion: twist the two cords in the hand by shifting the cord on the *right* side of the hand, *over* the other cord in the same hand (Fig. 7). Learn to do this with both hands simultaneously. Return hands to basic position with bobbins in new positions.

Fig. 5

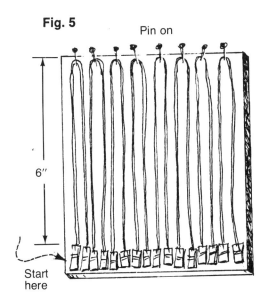

Pin on

6″

Start here

Fig. 6

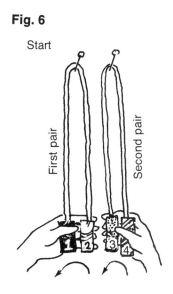

Start

First pair

Second pair

41

The other basic motion crosses cord from one hand over to the other. Shift the inside cord in left hand *over* inside cord in the right hand, while transferring the inside cord in right hand to left hand (Fig. 8). The cord from the left hand always goes *over* the cord from the right hand.

Master these basic motions—soon they become easy and automatic. The rest of the craft is learning various combinations and angles to work the cords. Always remember, a twist goes from right to the left, the cross goes

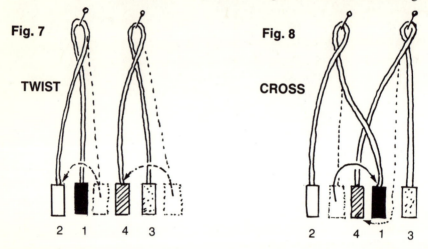

Fig. 7

TWIST

2 1   4 3

Fig. 8

CROSS

2   4 1   3

over to the right, and this *never* changes, no matter in which direction work progresses, even when coming back from the other side.

Practice, alternating motions; twist, cross over; twist, cross (see chart Fig 9): this will form a braid. Cross, twist, cross, twist—this is considered one complete (whole) stitch. One cross, twist is a half stitch (see chart Fig.9).

Braid first two pairs. Lay down the bobbins (always keep in order) and pick up next two sets of bobbins; make another braid. Continue across. It takes two pairs (four cords) to make a braid. By now you should be familiar with the basic motions. Give final twist on each braid before starting next stitch.

A mesh (or ground) is formed by working alternate pairs. Pick up adjacent pairs; B pair in left hand; C pair in right hand (Fig. 10). Work one complete stitch (cross, twist, cross, twist). Lay down these bobbins. Add pins at each intersection to maintain shape. Take up next two pairs: D and E. Continue across, working each adjacent pair. Starting at left again, give two twists to pair A (to compensate for not being working in previous row). Work stitches with alternate pairs—pair A and pair C (which is now adjacent). Continue across, B/E, D/F (Fig. 11), etc. Make several rows forming a mesh (Fig. 12). Mesh shape can be varied with more stitches between or using a half stitch each time.

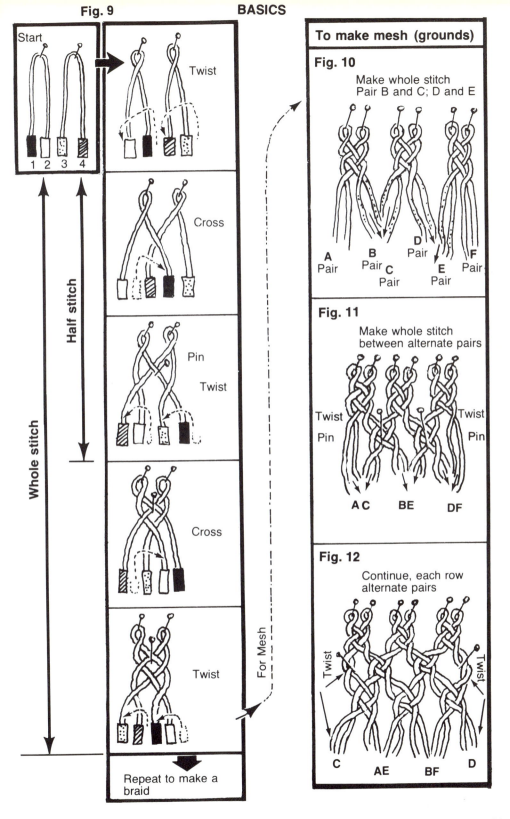

Fig. 9

BASICS

Start

1 2 3 4

Twist

Cross

Pin

Twist

Cross

Twist

Half stitch

Whole stitch

Repeat to make a braid

For Mesh

To make mesh (grounds)

Fig. 10

Make whole stitch
Pair B and C; D and E

A Pair

B Pair

C Pair

D Pair

E Pair

F Pair

Fig. 11

Make whole stitch
between alternate pairs

Twist

Pin

Twist

Pin

A C

B E

D F

Fig. 12

Continue, each row
alternate pairs

Twist

Twist

C

A E

B F

D

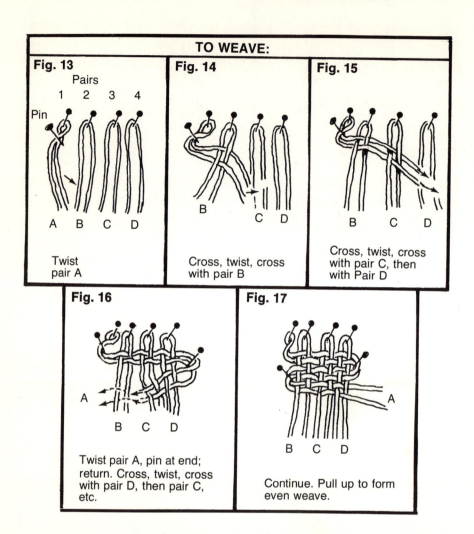

TO WEAVE:

Fig. 13

Pairs

1 2 3 4

Pin

A B C D

Twist
pair A

Fig. 14

B

C D

Cross, twist, cross
with pair B

Fig. 15

B   C   D

Cross, twist, cross
with pair C, then
with Pair D

Fig. 16

A

B C D

Twist pair A, pin at end;
return. Cross, twist, cross
with pair D, then pair C,
etc.

Fig. 17

A

B C D

Continue. Pull up to form
even weave.

Use these basic motions to create a woven area. As you work, one pair of bobbins is shifted sideways and becomes the weaving cords. To start, twist left pair (A); add pin at left (Fig. 13). Pick up first two pairs of bobbins (A) on left. Work weavers *horizontally* to the right. Use weaving stitch of three motions: cross, twist, cross (Fig. 14). Lay down pair of bobbins in left hand, shift weaving pair to left hand, and pick up next set of bobbins in right hand. Repeat the weaving stitch. Continue with each pair across and you will find the two cords (pair A) are woven between the rest (Fig. 15).

When completely across to right, give weaver pair of bobbins one twist, pin (Fig. 16), and start back, again horizontally. Make weaving stitch with adjacent pair. This time put pair in right hand down and shift weaver pair to right hand. Pick up next pair to left in left hand. Motions always remain the same—twist left, cross right. Practice weaving several rows until it comes easily to you. Pull up cords as necessary to form a neat woven area (Fig. 17).

As you use up cord, slip out of slit on bobbin, unwind, and slip back into slit. The weaver cord is used up more rapidly. If possible, plan a longer cord for the weaver. An extra twist in the work can exchange a hanging cord for a weaver cord that is becoming too short.

From these basic motions and stitches, most designs can be formed. Use two color cords to see how cords travel as they are worked. Try various stitch combinations and weaving at various angles with several weavers. There are many ways of forming various designs. Some complex patterns use a great number of bobbins. Eight pairs is a good starting number, but any number (usually multiples of four) can be used.

Once you have mastered the stitches, try making a wall hanging (see photo page 39).

MATERIALS
Cord; bobbins; backing board; tacks; pins; beads (optional).

The finished piece can be displayed on the board it was worked on or can be removed to hang. If board is to be part of design, cover with fabric to accent color of cords or use piece of weathered wood or cork. Mount cords on board with decorative tacks. If it's to hang without backing, mount cords on a stick, rod, or piece of driftwood.

Cut cords about four times the length of planned unit. Cords to make a wall decoration should be about ⅛″ thick—macrame cord, jute, or twine. Or use a nylon or polyester braid cord (from dime store); see photo. Beads with large holes, sold for macrame, can be added to design if desired. Slip beads on cords before winding on bobbins. If cords are firm enough, it may be possible to work the same motions without the bobbins. The finer the cords or threads, the more essential the bobbins.

After mounting the cords, plan a design to suit the weight of the cord. Fig. 1 is a suggestion. Use any combination of practiced basics. Work braids and mesh, for instance.

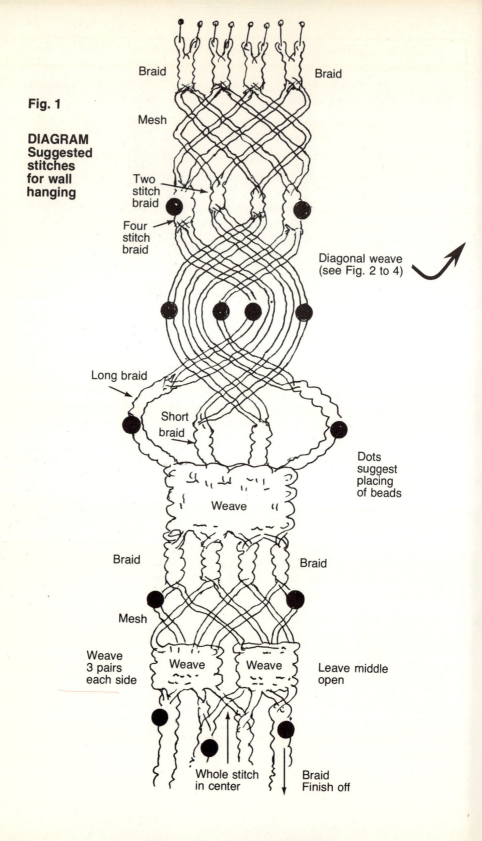

Fig. 1

DIAGRAM Suggested stitches for wall hanging

Braid

Braid

Mesh

Two stitch braid

Four stitch braid

Diagonal weave (see Fig. 2 to 4)

Long braid

Short braid

Dots suggest placing of beads

Weave

Braid

Braid

Mesh

Weave 3 pairs each side

Weave

Weave

Leave middle open

Whole stitch in center

Braid Finish off

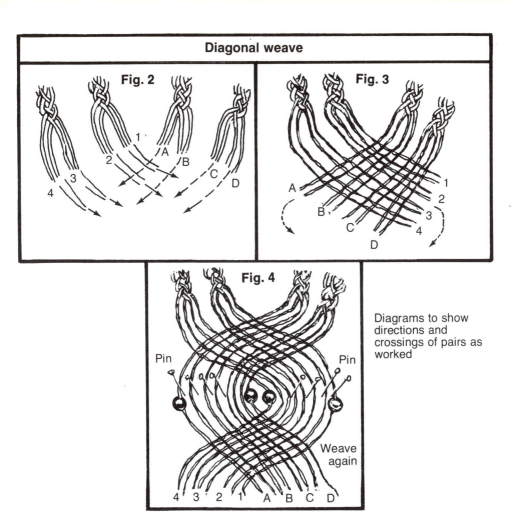

Diagonal weave

Fig. 2

Fig. 3

Fig. 4

Pin

Pin

Diagrams to show directions and crossings of pairs as worked

Weave again

4 3 2 1 A B C D

The center diagonal weave shown in Fig. 1 is a little more complex, as all pairs weave across each other. Start with the two center pairs (Fig. 2). Pick up pairs 1 and A, work weaving stitch (cross, twist, cross). Pin. Lay down A, shift pair 1 to left hand, and pick up pair B. Weave pair 1 on right. Then pick up pair 2 and work through pair A, then B, C, and D. Continue with pair 3 and then pair 4, angling each weaver pair to the right (Fig. 3). Pin and pull or shift cords as necessary to make a neat pattern.

Then weave all back again, angling as before. Center cords are now pairs D and 4. Make twist in each, add a bead to one cord of each pair if desired. Weave each pair across, repeating previous process; cords on left weave through all cords from right.

Before you start weaving back again, pin cords to maintain a curve at outside edges (Fig. 4). This weave shown is open and decorative. (At other times, the same weave can be pulled tighter together to make a dense area known as a spider).

After completing Fig. 4, make longer braids on each side, two inside braids shorter. Curve each long braid around and work in (see Fig. 1). Add more rows of mesh and weaving. To create an open area (see lower section Fig. 1), weave each side only to middle. Continue braids or mesh until desired length is achieved for wall hanging. If weaving cords become too short, splice on new lengths of cords (Fig. 5).

To finish the end of a braid, loop one of the ends (Fig. 6), wrap around other three strands, slip end in loop, and pull up to knot (Fig. 7). Add more beads, if desired. Trim ends. Add drop of glue if beads tend to slide out of position. A bead can finish an end. Or add a drop of glue to end of each cord to keep ends from raveling. Nylon line can be carefully scorched with a match to prevent raveling.

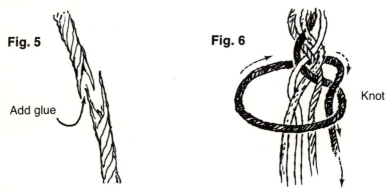

Fig. 5

Add glue

Fig. 6

Knot

This piece used three basic stitches—weaving, braid, and mesh—and only eight bobbins. Try starting with more bobbins, or add cords in as you work (Fig. 8), for different effects. Try various materials: stiffer things, like colored wire or fishline; crochet cotton or finer cords to make decorations for clothing and accessories. The variations are endless. Do explore the possibilities of contemporary bobbin lace.

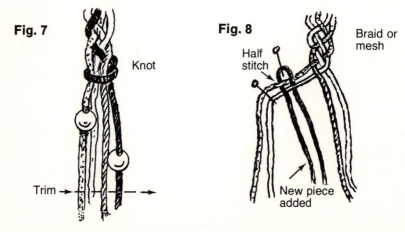

Fig. 7

Knot

Trim →

Fig. 8

Half stitch

Braid or mesh

New piece added

2

MOSAICS

A cave dweller arranging a few attractive pebbles in a pleasing design—was this the origin of mosaics? Through the years, throughout the world, stones and other materials were set together to make patterns. Floors and roads were made of shaped stones, marble, and other materials. The most durable and attractive floors were frequently mosaics. Roman and Etruscan mosaics were created by highly trained craftsmen, their skill held in great esteem. Some examples of their work are still in existence. Ornate mosaic designs covered not only floors but ceilings, walls, and ornamental pieces.

Tesserae:

The pieces of marble, glass, or stones used to make a mosaic were known as *tesserae* (singular *tessera*), from the Latin word meaning "cube" or "square." As Italian craftsmen became skilled in making these pieces, improving quality and variety of colors, mosaics became more complex and beautiful. These squares were often set onto the background at slight angles to add texture and reflect back the light for planned effects.

Religious Mosaics:

By the fourth century, mosaics were used to create large religious scenes and other church decorations, especially in Rome, Naples, and Milan. The Ravenna mosaics of the sixth century are considered the most splendid ever created. From the twelfth to fourteenth centuries, outstanding examples of mosaic work were done in many Italian cities. For the work in St. Peter's Cathedral in the sixteenth century, Muzio da Brecia invented a slower drying cement to enable craftsmen to do more elaborate work.

Painting came more into favor as a means of decoration during the

Renaissance, but magnificent mosaics still exist throughout Italy. The Vatican today maintains one of the largest mosaics studios, with a great variety of both old and modern tesserae available for repair work.

Some of the greatest mosaics ever created can be seen in Ravenna. This is a view of the Basilica of San Vitale.

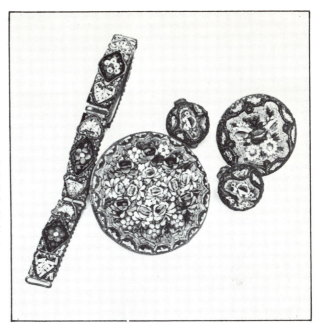

Examples of Italian miniature mosaics. The individual glass pieces are often colored or shaded in a way that adds to the delicacy of the overall design.

Miniatures:

For centuries, skilled Italian craftsmen have been making miniature mosaics—mostly jewelry, but also small ornamental objects such as picture frames. Minute pieces of glass tesserae are combined with glass rods sliced to size and *filato* (thin threads) of metal set between the sections. So fine is this work that a magnifying glass is often used in its creation.

Folk Art:

Italians, daily surrounded by great examples of mosaic work, probably wished they could embellish their own humble surroundings in some way. In many areas, to clear soil for gardening, all sorts of old marble, broken tiles, and old tesserae had to be removed. Sometimes these were salvaged and set in a blank cement wall to ornament a courtyard.

Famous examples of folk art, mosaics of shells and crockery, were made by an Italian immigrant to this country. Simon Rodia was about ten or twelve years old when he came to the United States, and by the time he died in 1954, the towers he had created had become famous. For thirty years he worked, covering steel rods with cement and embedding shells, tiles, broken

This detail shows a contemporary mosaic being constructed in a studio in Ravenna.

glass, and bottles (especially the green bottoms of 7-UP). A poor man, he gathered his material from dumps and the seashore. Spiraling 100 feet high, these incredible towers still stand in the Watts area of Los Angeles.

Mosaic Methods:

Several types of tesserae are now available to craftsmen. Highly glazed ¼″ squares are carried by most craft stores, but these are rather difficult to cut and too uniform in appearance. Smalti is Venetian glass in small, somewhat irregular squares. Various ceramic tiles have a high glaze, over a matte surface. Made for craftsmen, they cut easily. Vitreous tiles, used for commercial installation (countertops and bathrooms), are usually about 3/16″ thick. Most hobby tools will not cut this thickness; however, some thinner ones can be scored and then broken.

Random cut

Contour Pattern

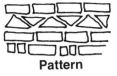
Pattern

Random square

In the broad sense, any piece of material (glass, shells, seeds, stones, marbles, wood pieces, etc.) that retains its own outlines yet creates a design when set on a surface could be called a mosaic.

Tesserae are attached to a background that is firm enough to support the weight of the applied mosaics. For small projects, masonite, pressed board, or plywood are good backings.

Tesserae can be set in any of the classic patterns, such as those shown. After a design is planned, pieces are attached with a glue or cement. When the glue sets, a grout (a type of fine cement) is mixed and worked in all the areas between the tiles. The surface is then cleaned. Briefly, this is how mosaics are made.

At a mosaic school in Ravenna, a young girl selects tessera to complete a mosaic. The painted sketch for the piece is on the left, behind the mosaic in progress.

Midden Mosaics

*Broken and cracked dishes recycled: the sconce was
made over a wooden base from a craft store; a
metal frame was the base for the mosaic trivet. A
small flower pot was covered with tiny mosaic pieces.*

Spread the word that you will accept everyone's broken dishes. At
garage sales and bazaars, haggle for usually unsalable items such as badly
chipped or cracked dishes. Soon you'll have enough to start making
mosaics. Flat, delicate china dishes of similar thickness with bright floral
or gold designs are best.

MATERIALS

Broken china; ceramic tiles (from craft store) to fill in color (optional).

Tile cutter-nipper (available at craft stores); hammer; base (to
attach tiles to); waterproof glue; grout (available at hardware
stores); disposable cups (for mixing grout); rags; grocery bag;
metal file.

A few of the possible uses for this mosaic technique are shown in the photo. Any firm surface—such as wood, metal, rigid plastic, or pottery—can be used for a base. Decide what to make: a tray, trivet, picture frame, bookend, sconce, planter. Craft stores carry metal backing shapes (trivets and ashtrays mostly) to hold tiles and boxes with recessed tops and other wooden forms. Or you could transform old discarded pieces such as a tray or a flowerpot.

Sort out your collection of broken china. Decide on a color scheme. There should be a certain unity of color, not just scattered pieces of various bright colors. Several plates of a set might be used to create border design or a central motif.

To break the china, place in a heavy double brown bag. Hit gently with a hammer and check to see what has broken Always break china inside a bag. Be careful of flying chips, sharp points. Some dishes are more difficult to break than others; some break unpredictably. It's better to discard an obstinate plate and use another. Some shards are sharper than others, but many are not sharp at all. Discard ridges and other pieces that are obviously thicker. To break into smaller units with designs and colors desired, it's helpful to place piece in a clear plastic bag to see what happens as you break it.

Select parts that are of similar thickness and fairly flat. Use a tile cutter (nippers) to make the smaller refined shapes. Hold the tile (or china piece) and place between nippers as shown (Fig. 1), only partially in from the edge, not all across the piece. With a little practice you will be able to cut just the angle and shape you wish. Some plates, however, will never cut as expected.

Fig. 1

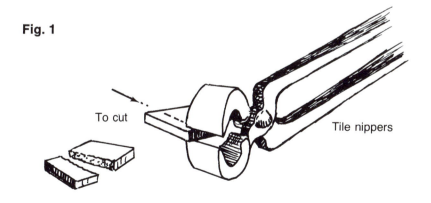

To cut

Tile nippers

As you cut, work with hands inside a clear plastic bag or wear goggles. Keep the working area clean. Do all cutting in a shallow box at the side, not on the work table area. The little discarded shards, if left lying around, can cut if you inadvertently put your elbow on them. Generally, edges of broken china pieces themselves are not sharp to handle, but be wary.

Cut pieces on a scale to the project you are doing. Small flowerpots could use tiny pieces less than ⅛″ across. Tweezers are helpful in placing these pieces. For larger units, use pieces about ¼″ to ½″ at widest dimension.

Plan design to best utilize the color and motifs of the pieces of china now cut. On a round tray, utilize curved edge design of broken plates (Fig. 2). Plan white areas between motifs to bring out the colors. (White is usually the most available color.) Purchased tiles can be used along edges or to add color in the design. However, they are not necessary.

Lay a piece of paper on the surface to be decorated; position the cut

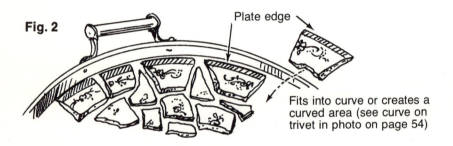

Fig. 2

Plate edge

Fits into curve or creates a curved area (see curve on trivet in photo on page 54)

tiles and china pieces. Cut as needed to fit. About ⅛″ space should be left between each edge (Fig. 3). This will vary of course, but try to allow for it, to create the character of mosaic. When satisfied with the arrangement, lift off the paper, being careful not to disturb the mosaic, and place next to base.

Now glue. Either spread glue on base and set tiles in, or add glue to each tile as it's placed. It may be necessary to trim a bit here and there as you fit pieces in place.

Fig. 3

⅛″ space

⅛″

If tiling a curved surface, such as a flowerpot, glue a small area at a time and let it dry. Then turn and do another section (Fig. 4). Allow glue to dry thoroughly.

In a disposable container, mix grout according to package directions. It should be about the consistency of thick cream (or a little thicker). Pour grout over the tiled surface and work it down into each crevice between each tile with a scrap of card or wood. Don't use fingers, since there may still be some sharp edges. When all crevices are filled, use a rag to wipe excess grout from the surface. Discard extra grout in the disposable cup—do not put it down the drain.

Let grout between tiles set. Check as it thickens and wipe surface again. When grout is thoroughly set and hard, use a damp cloth to wipe surface clean. Polish each tile so there is no grout film on tile. Each crevice between the tiles should be filled to tile level (Fig. 5).

In cleaning, you may find some edges are still somewhat protruding or sharp. When using broken dishes, it's not always possible to avoid that problem as there are slight curvatures in many places (Fig. 6). To remedy, use a metal file (from hardware store). Gently rub file across all possible sharp areas. Be careful not to scratch china surfaces. To complete, clean and polish your midden mosaic.

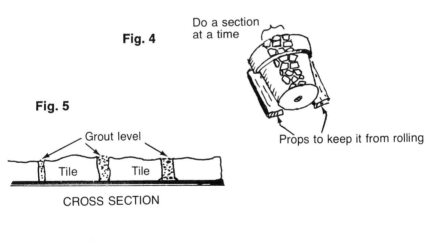

Fig. 4

Do a section at a time

Props to keep it from rolling

Fig. 5

Grout level

Tile   Tile

CROSS SECTION

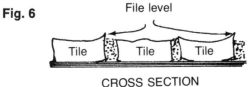

Fig. 6

File level

Tile   Tile   Tile

CROSS SECTION

Potshard Pendants

Shards that have become pendants: in the center is a saucer shard with gold leaf designs; the floral on the right was the center of large plate.

In breaking up the china, you may find you have some especially attractive designs and shapes. Save these and make some unusual pendants.

MATERIALS

Pieces of broken dishes about 2″ square (or any similar shape and size); metal file; jewelry findings; bell cap; link chain (or thong); glue; acrylic paint (optional); brush and clear nail polish (optional).

For a pendant, select a broken piece of plate of an appropriate size that shows an interesting piece of design. Trim slightly, if necessary, with tile nippers (see previous project). File all edges, making sure they are completely smooth. If design needs a little additional color, or looks a bit incomplete (Fig. 1), paint on extra designs using acrylic paint with matching or complementary color. Possibly paint the edges with matching color, or carry design around edge (Fig. 2). After paint is dry, cover with a coat of clear nail polish.

Jewelry findings and how to use them are described in Chapter 7. To make the shard into a pendant, use a bell cap. Fold bell cap around top of piece. Attach, using household cement or clear epoxy glue. When glue is set, attach to chain with a link (Fig. 3). Or slip a larger link over thong and tie on.

Fig. 1

Fig. 2

Paint on design

Paint edges

Fig. 3

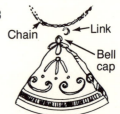

Chain

Link

Bell cap

Mini-Mosaics

The miniature mosaic effect on these pendants was easily created with colored broken eggshells.

The incomparable Italian miniature mosaic jewelry usually has silver wire dividers between areas of tiny glass mosaic pieces. The effect can only be created by skilled craftsmen using these materials, but it can provide inspiration to make some fun mosaic jewelry using eggshells.

MATERIALS
Eggshells; pendant frame; gold (or silver) cord or foil from candy wrappers or florist pots; food coloring or dyes; cardboard; gold or foil cardboard (backing of old Christmas card); white glue (that dries clear); toothpick; tweezers; plastic coating or clear nail polish; bead or glass rod slice (optional).

These mosaics look best in some sort of frame. There are several possible sources. Frames to hold coins or cameo frames are available from jewelry suppliers (see Chapter 7). Or you may find some old costume jewelry at sales, with a plastic ''cameo'' that can be removed to obtain an area to fill. Or any pendant or brooch with an open center can be decorated. The teardrop shape in the photograph was an outdated peace symbol. In this case the mosaic was glued over the symbol. Some shade pulls make suitable pendant frames (look in curtain departments of stores).

Save eggshells (not hardboiled). Prepare them by washing them and peeling off the inner membrane. Break into pieces about ½" across. Soak in dye, making several pieces of different colors. Allow colors to dry, keeping sorted according to color.

Separate color areas with tinsel cord (from craft store; see also ornaments in Chapter 6). Or use a foil strip to match frame. Cut a strip of foil

Fig. 1

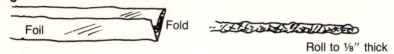

Foil   Fold   Roll to ⅛" thick

about ½" wide and fold over three times (Fig. 1), keeping color to outside. Then fold more and roll (like making "snakes" when working clay), making as thin a strip as possible. Strip should be less than ⅛" thick.

Fig. 2

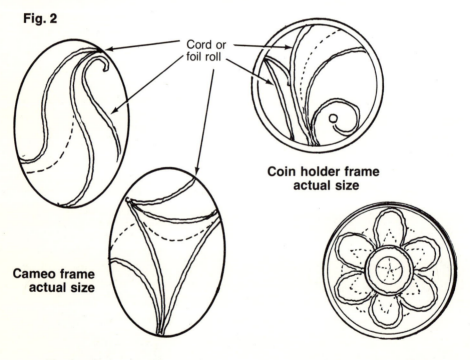

Cord or foil roll

Coin holder frame
actual size

Cameo frame
actual size

For backing, trace the opening of frame or trace around the "cameo" if one was removed. Cut this shape out of lightweight gray cardboard. Draw on the card a simple division of the area to be filled with mosaic. A few suggestions are shown in Fig. 2.

Solid lines indicate placement of cord or foil strips; dotted lines, a change of color without dividers. Decide on color scheme. Place glue,

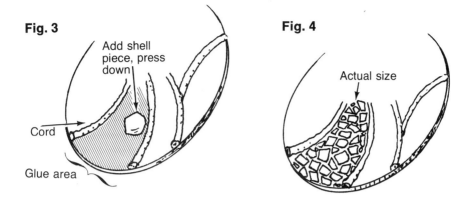

Fig. 3

Add shell piece, press down

Cord

Glue area

Fig. 4

Actual size

position a piece of cord (or foil strip), and trim to proper length. Add glue to area (Fig. 3), take piece of desired color eggshell, break into pieces about ¼″ across. Place in the glue, curved side up. Press down until shell cracks into smaller pieces. With a toothpick (or awl or any pointed tool), slide pieces slightly apart, so a fine line of the background can be seen between each piece. Break shell as necessary (Fig. 4) to create a mosaic look. Repeat in each area to complete design. Tweezers may be helpful in positioning cord and shell pieces.

When glue is dry, glue cardboard into frame. If frame has an open back, cut a flat piece of foil or gold cardboard to fit, and glue in back. A gold cord or foil strip around outside front edge may improve appearance, depending on type of frame. When all glue is dry, cover mosaic with a clear coating, such as nail polish.

A tiny interesting bead can be incorporated into the design, or a slice of glass rod. These slices are sold in craft stores for making copper enamel jewelry and have a design in each slice of the rod (Fig. 5), similar to those used in Italian jewelry. These are not necessary, but if available, they make a good focal point in the design.

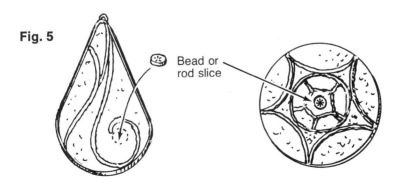

Fig. 5

Bead or rod slice

3

LEATHER

The Italians have always appreciated leather. By Roman times, processing of leather was well developed. Turning a stiff hide into a supple, workable state is known as tanning. The Latin word *tanare* means "oak bark." The tanning process involves soaking hides in a solution of bark and roots.

Roman shields were made by shaping leather over wooden forms. The tents of their armies were often made of leather. At one time Romans even used leather pieces as money.

In ancient times leather was essential for shelter, clothing, and for the basic strap. These strips of leather were needed for essential trappings, oxen

These examples of Italian carved and tooled leather-covered objects are from the sixteenth century.

harness, and reins and harnesses for horses. The strap held together possessions, and held armor in position. A faulty strap could be fatal if the armor slipped at a crucial moment in battle. Garments, cloaks, and head, hand, and feet coverings all were made of leather from Roman times to present.

Leather Guilds:

By the Middle Ages, skilled leather craftsmen belonged to guilds. The methods of tanning, shaping, and decorating leather all were carefully guarded secrets. Much of the work was done for the Church.

By the sixteenth and seventeenth centuries, leather items, often with ornate designs, were made for the nobles as well as the church. Gold tooling on leather was developed. Leather was used not only for practical purposes, saddles, harnesses, and cushions, but also for ornaments and furnishings, as well as book bindings. Desk tops and library tables of the Renaissance had leather inlaid tops. Boxes, jewel cases, door screens, even walls were leather paneled. These panels were tooled, often with biblical or mythological scenes.

Folk Craft:

For the peasant, leather was a plentiful material he used in many ways, plain or decorated. Buckets were made of leather. Furniture that might have been crudely made of poor wood was covered with leather. Leather pouches and bags were used to carry and store belongings.

Since glass was a luxury, leather flasks for liquids were made by shaping leather over forms, then sewing the shapes together. Pitch or resin was added inside to make them waterproof.

Leather Techniques:

The nobles had richly embossed leather flasks, sometimes with glass lining. This shaping and embossing was also used to make quivers and cases to hold various items. What was known as Venetian leather was not embossed; the surface was covered with gold leaf, then designs were incised. Color glazes were added in various parts of the design. Florentine leather was deeply embossed.

Most known methods of leathercrafting were used creatively by the Italians. On thick leather, lines were tooled, carved, or incised. Leather was stamped, molded, painted.

Leather Bank

With a bit of chamois leather, a discarded plastic container became a turtle bank, and a bottle that once held dressing for salad was transformed into a vase.

Chamois skin, available in most hardware and variety stores, is real leather. It's good to use to shape around forms. Although it cannot be tooled or embossed like heavy leather, you can create raised designs using the method below.

MATERIALS
Chamois skin; round plastic container with top, about 4″ diameter, 2″ high (such as soft margarine container); 2 plastic spoons; string; paper for patterns; wax paper; white glue (such as Sobo); brown liquid shoe polish; paste wax (optional).

To create the turtle bank, first turn the container over and cut a 1″ x ¼″ slit in what is now the top (fig. 1). For head, tape together two plastic spoons, bowls facing together. The top of lower one should be about ¼″

inside tip of top one (Fig. 2). Cut a hole in one side of container large enough to insert the spoon handles (see Fig. 1). Insert handles; glue and tape in proper position to look like a turtle head (Fig. 3).

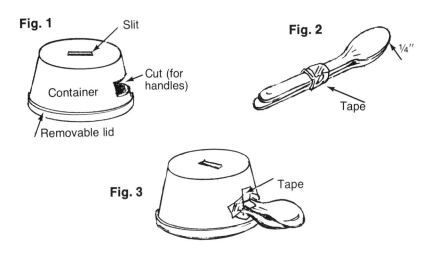

Fig. 1
Slit
Container
Cut (for handles)
Removable lid

Fig. 2
¼″
Tape

Fig. 3
Tape

Now it's ready to decorate. String will create the embossed design. Choose a sturdy string with firm, hard twist. Cut five 6″ pieces. Draw five spiral shapes around the slit (Fig. 4). Add a dab of glue to one area. Make a flat spiral of one string piece; set it into the glue. Allow to uncoil slightly. Lay a piece of wax paper over and press into the glue until it holds spiral shape. Remove paper and repeat, placing the five coils of string. For the sides, cut five more 6″ piece of string. Plan "S" coils. Draw on, spacing them around vertical sides (Fig. 4). Glue on these shapes, one at a time.

After glue dries, the next step is to cover entire unit. Make a paper pattern for each area to cover. Trace around top and slit area. Slit will be cut as shown (Fig. 5), folding small flaps in, along dotted lines. Make side

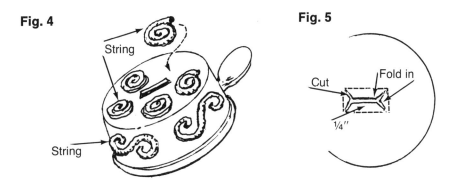

Fig. 4
String
String

Fig. 5
Cut
Fold in
¼″

Fig. 6   **Fig. 7**

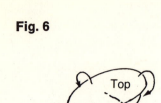

Make piece big enough
to fold under

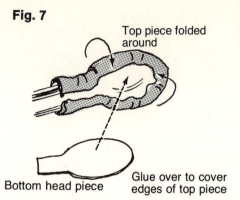

Top piece folded
around

Bottom head piece

Glue over to cover
edges of top piece

piece, ending and fitting around neck. Cover head with two pieces; top and sides of head, one piece (Fig. 6), underside of head another (Fig. 7). Trace foot pattern (Fig. 8). After drawing patterns, lay patterns on the chamois. If one part is thicker, use this section to cut the feet. Also plan for several strips about 18″ long, ⅛″ wide, for braid trimmings. Cut out pieces.

Apply chamois wet. Soak it, then wring it out thoroughly. Add glue to the top and lay on, add glue inside slit opening, fold edges down into slit and to inside (see Fig. 5). Press down and work the chamois around the string patterns. Chamois is flexible; it stretches when wet, shrinks when dry. As the glue and chamois dry, continue pressing and shaping until surface texture shows in every detail.

Fig. 8   **Fig. 9**

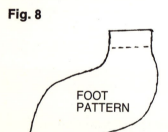

FOOT
PATTERN

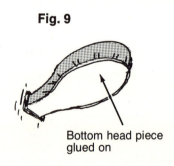

Bottom head piece
glued on

Next do the head, gluing on top piece (see Fig. 6), stretching it around sides, across the open space between the spoons, and under. Add glue along edges of folded around piece and underside of head. Glue on underside piece (see Fig. 7), overlapping edges of top piece already folded around lower spoon (Fig. 9). Head should be completely covered. Trim off any excess. Keep checking and stretching as it dries.

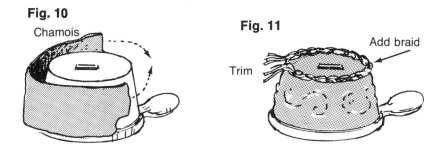

Fig. 10

Chamois

Fig. 11

Add braid

Trim

Cover side of body (Fig. 10), overlapping slightly by neck. Keep pressing to bring out design. Trim to fit around neck. Glue chamois to base piece so entire circle is leather covered, no plastic showing.

Cut three ⅛″ strips of chamois about 16″ long or more, to braid into a piece long enough to go around top edge of turtle. Wet the strips, then braid. Add glue to braid and glue around top edge (Fig. 11), trimming where ends

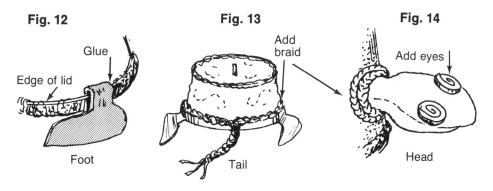

Fig. 12

Glue

Edge of lid

Foot

Fig. 13

Add braid

Tail

Fig. 14

Add eyes

Head

meet. Work ends into each other and glue, making a neat joining. Be careful not to get glue on any surface of leather that will show. Make another braid long enough to go just above the joining of the removable base. Glue feet in position (Fig. 12) around lip of base piece, then put base in place. Glue braid around lower edge, making sure at least half of the base can still be pulled off (to remove coins). All plastic should be covered.

For tail, make a 2″ braid and glue at base where ends of lower braid meet in back (Fig. 13), or use end of this braid for tail, if there is extra. Unravel about ½″ at end of tail, add glue to prevent further raveling. Make a 6″ braid, add glue, and wind twice around base of neck to hide joining. For eyes, cut two 2½″ strips of ⅛″ wide chamois. Add glue to a strip and wind up into a flat tight coil (Fig. 14). Repeat for other eye. Glue in position on head.

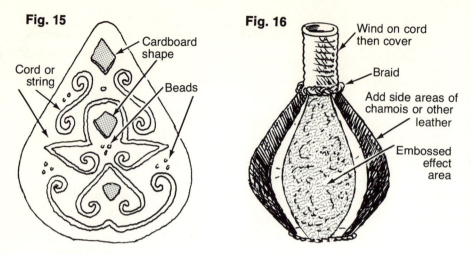

Fig. 15

Cardboard shape

Cord or string

Beads

Fig. 16

Wind on cord then cover

Braid

Add side areas of chamois or other leather

Embossed effect area

When all glue is dry, add color. Chamois is usually too pale to look like old leather. Generously apply liquid brown shoe polish, making sure all crevices and braids are colored. Wipe off excess on surface. If desired, wax unit when dry. Now bank can be filled with coins.

Other plastic containers, with a little imagination, can become animals or decorative banks with this "embossed leather" look. It's also effective on glass or plastic bottles. Plan a decorative area on a bottle and make a paper pattern. Glue on string designs. Pieces of card and small beads can also add dimension (Fig. 15). Glue onto bottle. Glue chamois over. Draw pattern for remaining areas to be covered (Fig. 16); cut and glue on chamois. Add braid trims where pieces meet. These brown-toned vases look effective filled with dried flowers (Fig. 17).

Fig. 17

Encased Bottles

Examples of discards turned elegant. On the left, a dime store sugar bowl became a handsome desk accessory with addition of green and brown suede triangles. On the right, shiny leather contrasts with rough suede.

There is a tactile quality and elegance to leather, even without the embossed look. If you have access to scraps of leather, try covering some interesting-shaped bottles.

MATERIALS
Scraps of various leathers (preferably not much more than 1/16″ thick); a bottle; glue (such as Sobo); lightweight paper; trimmings (optional).

Some craft stores carry assortments of scraps of leather. Or you can use leather from an old handbag, a discarded vest, or other useless garment. Chamois can be used for lighter color accents.

Clean the bottle and decide on a design. If scraps are very small, work existing shapes into the design, then fill between. Draw a pattern, planning on several pieces to cover area. Cut out nonadjacent areas (such as A, C, and E in Fig. 1). Dampen the leather, then apply glue. Place each leather piece on the bottle; press and stretch until each adheres. Because of some stretching, areas between will be different than original pattern. On paper, trace

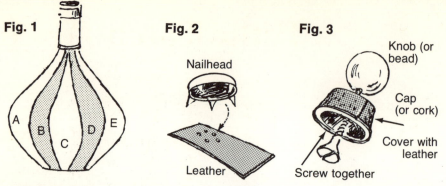

Fig. 1 **Fig. 2** **Fig. 3**

Nailhead

Leather

Knob (or bead)

Cap (or cork)

Cover with leather

Screw together

uncovered areas to make new pattern (such as areas B and D in Fig. 1). Cut out, wet leather, and glue on. As the leather stretches, it can curve around contours somewhat and be pulled to butt edges tightly. Slide pieces about until edges meet as desired and the glue holds. Work at it as the glue sets to make sure leather stretches and fits, as needed. Make patterns and add pieces up neck of bottle and on the base.

For trim, thin strips of leather can be added where edges of leather pieces meet. Or add braids of chamois or a strand of jute (or other such cord). A string of wooden beads could make an interesting trim around the bottle neck.

Nailheads (Fig. 2) also make appropriate decorations. Cut out leather piece according to plan. Push prongs of nailhead into leather to mark it. Make holes with an awl and push nailhead through leather; fold prongs back. Then glue the leather piece in place. Pieces from old jewelry can be glued on for ornaments.

For a top, cover original top with leather or screw in position a wooden knob or large bead (Fig. 3). The bottle shape may suggest ideas for decorating (Fig. 4). Not only bottles but all sorts of discards can be transformed by this method, to make desk accessories, decorative flowerpots, or boxes.

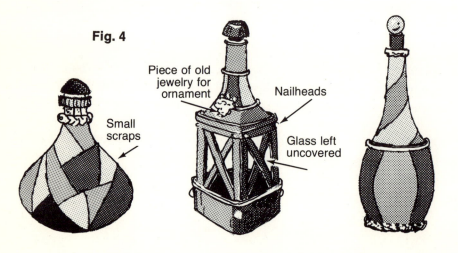

Fig. 4

Piece of old jewelry for ornament

Nailheads

Small scraps

Glass left uncovered

Petite Patch Pouch

Elbow patches were the source of leather for this tiny suede pouch bag. It can be attached to a belt or worn on a long cord over the shoulder.

Pouchmakers, or pursers, were members of special guilds. They made leather containers for carrying a person's money or possessions. Little hip purses were a fad for women in Florence around the eleventh century, and the style spread throughout Europe. Italian craftsmanship of bags is well known even today.

Hung from a belt or chatelaine, small receptacles had many names; purse, pouch, poke, bag, reticule. It was not until the last century that "handbags" came into existence. The little reticule was a charming fashion idea that is being revived today to carry small valuables close to oneself.

MATERIALS
2 sets of suede leather elbow patches; yarn; yarn needle; heavy thread; regular needle; fabric glue (such as Sobo); awl; small piece of corrugated cardboard; clip clothespins.
Acrylic paint; felt pen; small brush; paper (all optional).

Suede leather elbow patches are available in most stores that sell sewing accessories. Try to find those that have prepunched holes around the edges. Patches may vary in size, so adapt measurements as needed. Select a yarn that complements the color of the patch.

Cut the patches into the pieces indicated (Fig. 1). All edges—front, back, flap, and sides—will need holes punched (except base of side pieces). Lay a piece with a cut edge on cardboard. Using the awl, punch holes, spacing the same as prepunched holes. Repeat on all cut edges. If patches are not prepunched, punch all edges making holes about ¼" in from edge, ¼" apart.

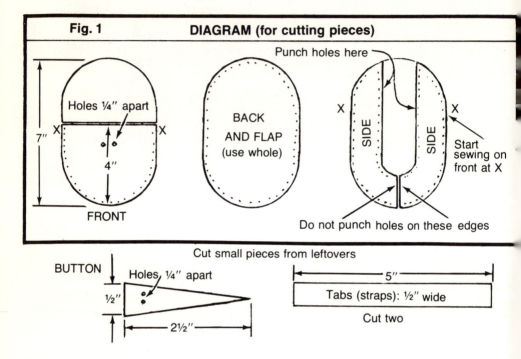

Fig. 1   **DIAGRAM (for cutting pieces)**

Holes ¼" apart
7"
4"
FRONT

Punch holes here

BACK AND FLAP (use whole)

X   SIDE   SIDE   X
Start sewing on front at X

Do not punch holes on these edges

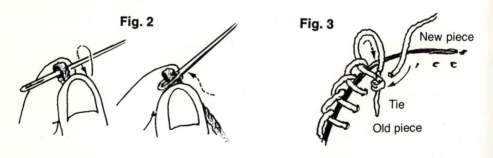

Cut small pieces from leftovers

BUTTON
Holes ¼" apart
½"
2½"

5"
Tabs (straps): ½" wide
Cut two

Thread needle with length of yarn. Fold yarn around needle by creasing it, then forcing crease through eye (Fig. 2). Use yarn double throughout. Buttonhole-stitch into holes; (see Chapter 7, Stitchery). Go around edge of each piece. At end of yarn, tie off in back (Fig. 3) and start a new piece. Add a dab of glue at tie; when dry, trim ends close.

Fig. 2

Fig. 3

New piece

Tie

Old piece

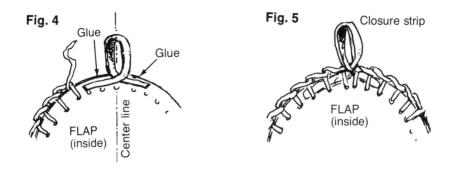

Fig. 4

Glue

Glue

FLAP
(inside)

Center line

Fig. 5

Closure strip

FLAP
(inside)

Before completing top center of flap, make a closure loop. Cut a strip 4″ long, ¼″ wide, from a leftover piece of leather. Glue end between holes and edge. Make a loop (Fig. 4) and glue other end. Hold with clip clothespin until dry. Then continue buttonholing around, allowing closure loop to hang from edge (Fig. 5).

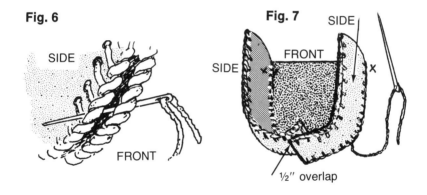

Fig. 6

SIDE

FRONT

Fig. 7

SIDE

FRONT

SIDE

½″ overlap

Now assemble pouch. With yarn and needle, attach pieces by going alternately into top of each buttonhole stitch (Fig. 6). Start by sewing side to front, matching X's in Fig. 1. Sew together, down nearly to bottom center. The amount of overlap of sides as they meet at base of bag (Fig. 7) can now be determined. Overlap may vary according to size of patch. Trim off, if necessary, so there is no more than ½″ overlap. Glue this overlap and allow glue to dry; then complete, attaching sides to front. Attach back in same manner. Starting at center bottom, sew back to sides, aligning with front piece. At top of side piece, go through existing holes with extra stitches to strengthen joining. Tie off, and add a bit of glue. Add glue on inside wherever yarn has had to be tied off.

To make button, cut piece size shown in Fig. 1. Make holes indicated. Add glue to wrong side, roll up tightly, and hold with clothespin until dry.

Or use any appropriate button. Fold flap over to determine position for button to fit closure loop. Place a card in bag; make holes with awl in front of bag. Remove card. With heavy thread, sew on button.

For hanging strap (tabs), cut two pieces 5″ x ½″. Fold in half and glue as shown (Fig. 8). Make distance A-B longer to wear with a wider belt. Punch holes indicated. In top of side of bag, punch corresponding holes (Fig. 9). Thread 6″ piece of yarn on needle; use it doubled. Place strap on inside

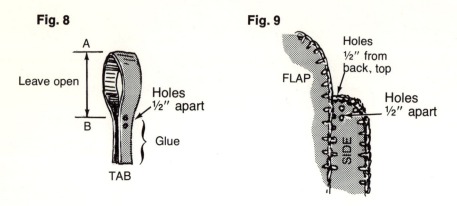

Fig. 8

A

Leave open

B

Holes
½″ apart

Glue

TAB

Fig. 9

Holes
½″ from
back, top

FLAP

Holes
½″ apart

SIDE

of bag, push needle in from outside, through double thickness of strap, and back out again. Cut off yarn near needle (Fig. 10); tie ends. Cut two 3″ pieces of yarn; tie into yarn ends. To make these hanging yarns into a tassel, thread needle with regular thread, sew through knot, then wind around hanging ends just below knot (Fig. 11). Tie thread, cut off, trim tassel ends. Repeat on other side.

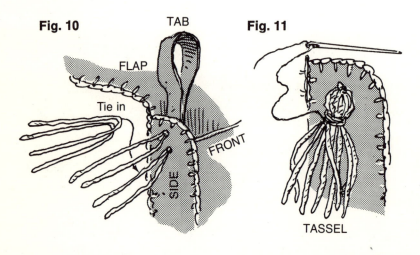

Fig. 10

TAB

FLAP

Tie in

FRONT

SIDE

Fig. 11

TASSEL

Glue lower ends of tabs to inside of bag for extra firmness. Slide belt through tabs. If preferred, make tabs smaller (A-B in Fig. 8), add a long chain or cord through loops (Fig. 12), and wear over the shoulder.

If a decoration is desired: on paper, draw a design such as Fig. 13. Cut out shape. Lay purse flap flat, lay paper pattern on flap, and trace through opening in paper, drawing design onto the suede (Fig. 14). Remove paper and carefully paint decoration, using acrylic paint or felt marker to color in.

If preferred, the petite pursette could be made of leather from a craft store. Make patterns to determine how much will be needed (patches are about 5″ x 7″ each). Or use leather from an old soft handbag or discarded vest. Or instead, it coud be made of felt or sturdy fabric. How about some trapunto trim? Sew regular seams if using fabric.

Fig. 12

Fig. 13

DESIGN Actual size
(trace if desired)

Fig. 14

Paper

Cut out

FLAP

4

WOOD AND STRAW

Very early, man learned that he could use a sharp tool to notch a dry branch. The notches might have had meaning or merely been decorative. The origin of woodcarving is very ancient.

Carving:

Italians carved designs into all kinds of wood surfaces. The shepherd passing time with his flocks carved his staff. The cart, oxen yoke or milking stool were often carved. Many of the designs were simple chip-carved geometrics, but some were carved reliefs of rural scenes, animals, and floral designs. Initials, sentimental designs, and religious motifs were used in the carvings, as well as some of the more ancient symbols of the sun and moon.

Toys were usually carved of wood. Furniture, cupboards, cradles, utensils, tools, and especially the wedding chest (*cassone*) had carved de-

A large wooden cassone *from early fifteenth century Florence has painted areas depicting mythological scenes.*

A seventeenth century carved wood chair from northern Italy shows some basic chip carved motifs.

signs. As each bride traditionally had such a chest, the designs often included hearts and other symbols of love. Sometimes painted designs were combined with the carving.

Carving was also a profession, and woodcarvers made elaborate work for the churches. Often monks were skilled at the craft. After the sixteenth century, professional carvers worked for the wealthy as well as the church. Furniture, paneling, boxes, portraits—many items were ornately carved.

Intarsia:

Inlay, an ancient method of decorating wood, was also known as intarsia *(intarsiato)*. A space was cut down into the surface of the wood and contrasting material cut to fit exactly into this space. Craftsmen of Venice and Lombardy became known for inlay work, especially of ivory and mother-of-pearl. Barili of Sienna (1453–1546) was known for his minutely detailed inlay of floral and religious designs.

An example of fifteenth century architectural
woodwork from the Ducal palace at Gubbio.
Inlaid wood on a flat surface creates the effect.
The diagram at the right shows the actual
structure of the room shown in the photograph.
No other dimension exists — no cupboards or
objects within them, no tables or organ pipes.
The entire illusion is created with the inlaid
wood. It is believed that this room was designed
by Francesco di Giorgio of Siena and made by
Baccio Pontelli of Florence.

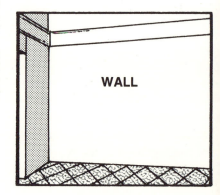

WALL

Marquetry-Parquetry:

A method was discovered in the sixteenth century to cut wood into very thin layers. These thin layers of exotic woods could be glued over plain but sturdy wooden pieces. Instead of having to use inlay to decorate wood, craftsmen could cut and assemble designs of various textures and colors of the thin woods and affix them to the heavier wood. This was known as marquetry. Parquetry, geometric designs of slightly heavier wood, was used primarily for floors.

Marquetry, in the hands of skilled workmen, had unlimited possibilities. All types of furniture were embellished. There are examples of rooms (studies) of the Renaissance period where the walls were covered with marquetry. Skilled marquetry craftsmen created the three-dimensional effect of cupboards with objects on the shelves, doors open or ajar on what was still a flat wall. The dimension was an illusion created by the assembled wood pieces. The Renaissance fascination with perspective was utilized by those who created with wood.

Straw Marquetry:

In every generation, the poorer folk desired to emulate the expensive crafted products available to the rich. With ingenuity, they often found substitutes such as straw, so readily available to farmers. Italians, inspired by the best wood marquetry, covered such items as sewing boxes with inlay straw designs. By the end of the eighteenth century fine examples of this craft were in demand by the wealthy.

Chip Carving

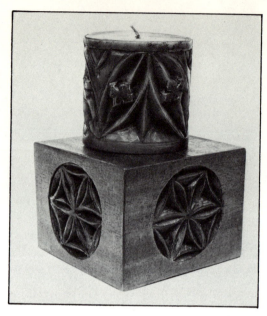

Both candle and base have been ornamented by chip carving.

Folk woodcarving often was chip carving. To become familiar with the technique, let's start with something soft and easy like a candle, then add a carved balsa wood base.

MATERIALS
Plain colored candle about 3″ high, 3″ diameter; knife, such as a penknife or X-acto; lightweight paper; acrylic paint (burnt umber); paintbrush.

Trace the solid lines of the design (Fig. 1) on paper. Trace other half of pattern. Repeat the motif three times in a 9¼″ x 3″ rectangle. Lay paper around the candle to make sure the three-unit design fits. Space or condense between each unit if necessary, repeating evenly around the candle. Tape pattern around candle and trace over design with a sharp pencil, checking that the candle surface is visibily indented. Remove the paper after tracing and clarify any lines that might not be distinct. Surfaces of commercial candles vary; some may be easier to mark and cut than others.

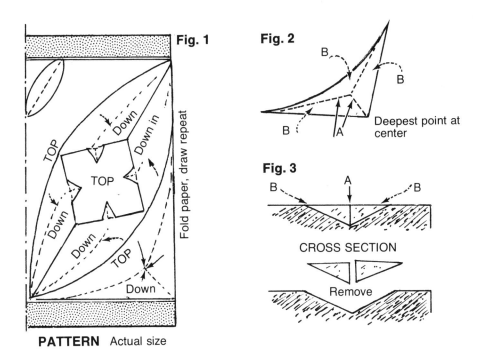

PATTERN Actual size

Chip carving depends on the angle of the knife. The dotted lines indicate vertical cuts (lines A, Fig. 2). Solid lines in pattern indicate angled cuts to intersect vertical cuts (lines B, Fig. 2), see also cross-section (Fig. 3). Properly done, a single clean cut on each line at the proper angle allows a piece to be removed. The center of the vertical cuts, in most cases, is deeper, tapering off to the corners.

For center motifs (Fig. 4), leave the square area in center on the surface. Then, in each side of square, cut notches to complete design (Fig. 5).

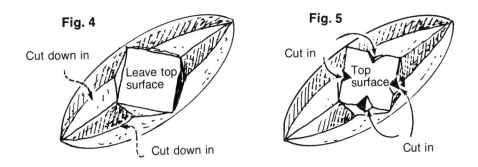

Carve the three repeats around the candle. With a brush, remove any crumbles. Ideally, cuts should be clean and accurate so no cleaning is necessary. Dilute burnt umber acrylic paint—or use any color darker than the color of your candle. Brush paint down into the carving. Allow paint to darken the recesses. Wipe off surface for an antique effect.

Now you can build a base for your candle.

MATERIALS

Balsa wood, 3″ x ½″, at least 14″ long; piece of veneer large enough to get four 3⅛″ x 4⅛″ pieces plus two 4⅛″ squares; 3″ x 3″ x 3″ block of rigid packing foam or Styrofoam from craft store (or block of wood).

Knife, such as an X-acto; sandpaper; glue for wood and foam (such as Sobo); burnt umber paint (or wood stain); brush; paper for pattern; small nail (at least 1″ long) with head; awl; compass (optional).

This candle base is a block covered first with Balsa, which carves easily, then with a thin veneer to create the look of a block of quality wood. Veneer is avalable in some lumberyards or by mail order (see Chapter 7). Some hardware or lumberyards carry rolls of veneer for finishing edges; if veneer sheets are not available, get the widest width and piece it together for this project.

Cut the balsa wood into four pieces, each 3″ x 3½″ (Fig. 1). They should fit exactly around the rigid foam cube, one end grain showing on each side. Trace the heavy line of the design (Fig. 2) on paper and draw the other half. This basic chip-carved design goes back to antiquity and is carved from identical circles.

Fig. 1

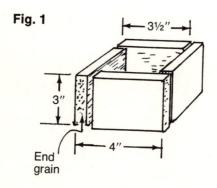

3½″

3″

End grain

4″

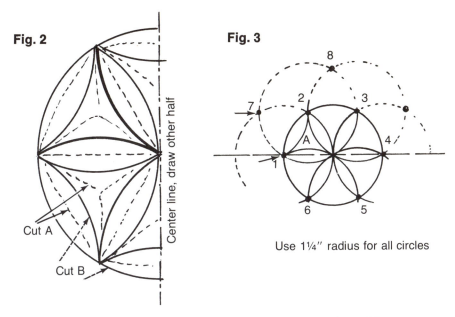

Fig. 2

Cut A

Cut B

Center line, draw other half

Fig. 3

8

7

2

3

A

4

1

6

5

Use 1¼″ radius for all circles

If you wish to get more accurate circles, redraw design with a compass (Fig. 3). Draw a basic circle, place compass at point 1, draw circle, continue to point 2, etc. Center point for curve A can be found by extending each drawn circle and placing compass at outside intersecting points (point 7).

With a soft pencil, blacken back of drawing, place on a piece of Balsa wood. Position as shown, centerpoint 2″ from right edge (Fig. 4). When cube is assembled, circle will be centered. Transfer design onto the wood.

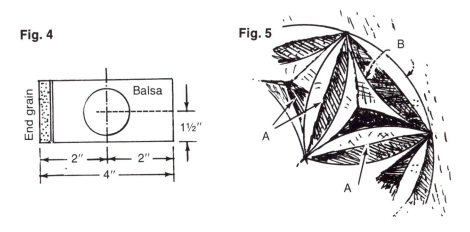

Fig. 4

End grain

Balsa

1½″

2″   2″

4″

Fig. 5

B

A

A

Carve the design, using the same method as for the candle, making vertical cuts (A) on dotted lines (Fig. 5) and angled cuts (B) to meet vertical cuts. Repeat on all four balsa wood pieces. Clean out any loose particles.

Fig. 6

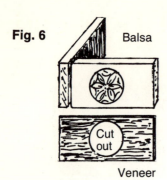

Balsa

Cut out

Veneer

Fig. 7

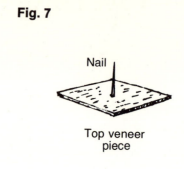

Nail

Top veneer piece

As balsa is too blond to look like quality wood, use thinned paint (or wood stain) and paint all carved areas, being careful not to get it too dark or to obscure the wood look.

Cut four pieces of veneer 3⅛″ x 4⅛″. On paper, draw area of side; trace outline of carved circle. This time the circle is centered, as the veneer will cover the end grain of adjacent side (Fig. 6). Trace onto veneer and cut out circle. Repeat on other sides. If using veneer strips, butt edges to make height needed.

Glue the balsa pieces to the cube, arranging as shown in Fig. 1, end grain at left on each side. When pieces are attached, glue the veneer pieces over, making sure circles fit around carved areas and end grain is covered. Glue on one piece at a time, weight down until glue dries. When the four sides are attached, draw outline for top and bottom pieces by placing unit on the veneer and tracing around edges. Cut top and bottom; glue bottom in place, aligning edges. Trim if necessary, and lightly sand all corners and edges.

In center of top piece, poke a small hole with awl. Push the nail up through (Fig. 7). Glue piece to top of the cube, with nail up, to hold the candle.

Brush away all loose dust. Lightly stain the veneer if desired. To finish, give it a coat of wax or varnish. With an awl, make a small hole in the bottom center of the candle, place on nail.

This base is adequate for 3″-high candle. If using a taller one, base should be weighted. Before gluing on bottom, cut away some of the foam cube, making an area for a rock (or piece of heavy metal). Glue in weight, then glue on the veneer bottom.

Once you are familiar with chip-carving methods, you might want to try pine or other softwood. Special knives for this type of woodcutting are available at craft suppliers.

Overlay: Bird Bookends

Purchased teak bookends were decorated with a design made from veneers, cut and overlaid.

Marquetry (inlay) involves fitting cut veneer pieces exactly against each other. A modern use of veneer is overlay, an easier method. To become familiar with veneer wood, try these bookends using the overlay method.

MATERIALS

Plain wooden bookends (from variety store); pieces of veneer, light wood—such as birch—and dark—such as walnut; decorative wood inlay border (optional).

Knife, such as a penknife or X-acto; white glue; fine sandpaper; weights; clear sticky tape.

Assortments of small veneer pieces, as well as decorative borders already inlaid with designs, are available by mail order from suppliers such as Constantine (see Chapter 7).

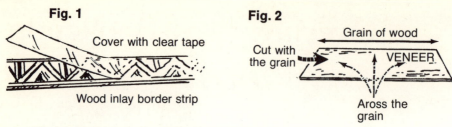

Fig. 1
Cover with clear tape
Wood inlay border strip

Fig. 2
Grain of wood
Cut with the grain
VENEER
Aross the grain

The decorative inlaid borders are sometimes fragile and may come apart. To hold together, stick a piece of tape over entire face (Fig. 1). Remove after piece is cut and glued into position. If surface remains sticky, clean with nail polish remover before sanding.

If you plan to make larger units or veneer furniture, you can purchase larger veneer pieces and then make smaller projects, such as this one, from trims. Choose contrasting woods such as birch and walnut or mahogany. If

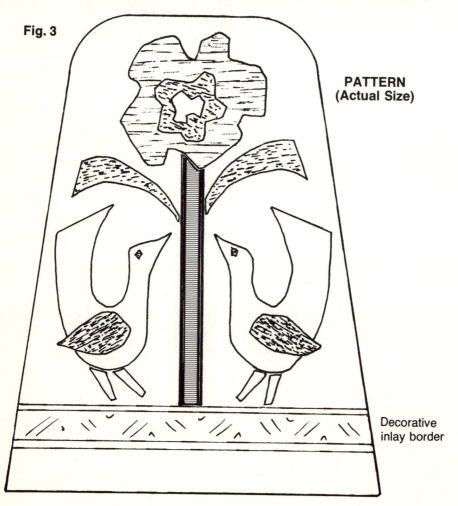

Fig. 3

PATTERN
(Actual Size)

Decorative inlay border

you wish more variety of color, the birch can be tinted with any dye, even food coloring. Orange or yellow are best as they suggest wood tones.

Try cutting a few scrap pieces of veneer to get the feel of the wood. Use a sharp knife. Be aware of the grain of the wood. Make long cuts with the grain (Fig. 2).

Wood can be dampened slightly to make it more pliable and less likely to split. Wet a cloth, wring and lay on wood briefly to allow moisture to penetrate piece.

If a break occurs with the grain, it can often be butted back together when gluing down and hardly be noticeable.

Cutting across the grain is more difficult (Fig. 2). It is better to use several short light strokes, going over a cut several times, rather than one heavy cut.

Now that you have the feel of the wood, trace the pattern (Fig. 3) or draw your own design. Cut shapes from veneers. For area below birds, cut a length of decorative veneer border or use three strips of wood, alternating colors. Stem can be a narrow decorative border or 3/16"-wide strip of dark wood. Cut ⅛" eyes of tiny scraps of dark wood. When the shapes are cut, smooth any rough edges gently with sandpaper.

Commercial teak bookends usually come already finished. If using unfinished wood, stain and sand. Glue first layer of veneer pieces in place, weight down, and let glue dry. Then add next layer (Fig. 4): the wings, flower (middle layer) and eyes. Add flower center last.

Fig. 4

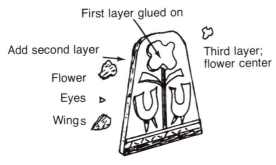

First layer glued on

Add second layer

Flower

Eyes ▷

Wings

Third layer; flower center

Sand lightly, if necessary. Finish unit with clear acrylic spray or spray varnish. Do not attempt to brush on a finish, as the coating may accumulate and lump along veneer edges.

This overlay method is good for plaques, pendants, boxes, or any flat, preferably vertical, surface.

Inlaid Veneers

A shallow wooden tray, an ordinary cutting board, and an old battered box — each was resurfaced with pre-inlaid borders combined with light and dark veneers.

Now try inlay. Any wood surface, old or new, can be transformed with the veneers and inlay borders available today.

MATERIALS

Wooden surface (such as a cutting board, box, tray or piece of plywood); pieces of veneer; decorative inlay borders; white glue or special veneer adhesive (see suppliers, Chapter 7).

T-square or workshop square; medium to fine sandpaper, steel wool; knife; masking or transparent sticky tape; rubber cement; paper; ruler; weights or clamps; varnish and brush, paste wax.

Plan a design for area you wish to inlay, utilizing veneers you may have. Veneer and border strips were discussed in previous project. Order other pieces that may be needed. It is possible to use wood edge strips available at local hardware or lumber dealers. Made to edge furniture, they come in several widths, with a paperlike backing. However, they are often slightly thinner than the veneer inlays, and extra sanding will be needed to make a smooth surface.

On paper, make an accurate drawing of design. For beginners, plan most areas to be straight edges which can be butted against each other (Fig. 1). Most cuts should be right angles. Cut veneer and strips to size.

Checkerboard areas are effective. Mark with T-square on the veneer, then cut strips using metal straightedge. Lay these strips next to each other,

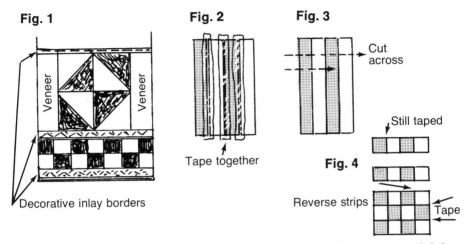

Fig. 1

Veneer

Veneer

Decorative inlay borders

Fig. 2

Tape together

Fig. 3

Cut across

Still taped

Fig. 4

Reverse strips

Tape

alternating light and dark. Place tape on right side to hold these strips tightly against each other (Fig. 2). Mark width of square. Using workshop metal square, cut across taped pieces (Fig. 3), making sure all cuts are absolutely square. Turn alternate strips (Fig. 4) to achieve a checkerboard. Remove tape after gluing in position.

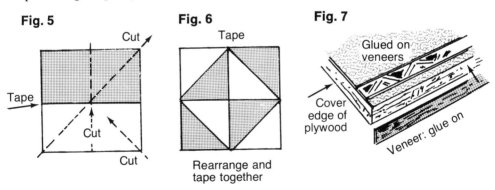

Fig. 5

Cut

Tape

Cut

Cut

Fig. 6

Tape

Rearrange and tape together

Fig. 7

Glued on veneers

Cover edge of plywood

Veneer: glue on

Triangles are made in a similar manner, by cutting across larger squares (Fig. 5). Rearrange contrasting colors (Fig. 6) to create design. Tape to hold together until ready to glue. If breaks occur, in some cases pieces can be taped to keep together until gluing.

If any special cuts or mitered corners are needed, cut paper pattern accurately along lines. Using rubber cement, attach pattern to the veneer. Cut precisely along pattern edge, then remove pattern.

Sand surface to be decorated and clean off. Using square, mark areas where design and borders will be placed. Glue on a section at a time, butting all edges tightly. If using glue, weight down or clamp until glue dries. Keep checking to make sure veneer is adhering properly. If using special adhesive, follow instructions on can.

Allow veneer to protrude slightly over edges if possible. When glue is thoroughly dry, trim and sand even with edge. If plywood was used for base wood, cut strips of veneer the thickness of the wood, and glue them along exposed edges (Fig. 7).

When all veneers are securely adhered to the surface, sand thoroughly, using a medium sandpaper. Then use finer and finer grades of sandpaper until top feels level and very smooth, without scratches. Finally, rub with steel wool. Remove any traces of dust.

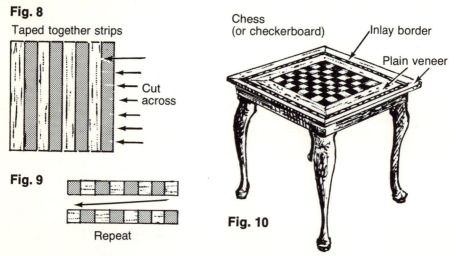

Fig. 8

Taped together strips

Cut
across

Fig. 9

Repeat

Chess
(or checkerboard)

Inlay border

Plain veneer

Fig. 10

Give several coats of varnish. When varnish is thoroughly dry, rub with steel wool to achieve a rich mellow surface. Wood can then be finished with paste wax and buffed.

After making a small unit, you might wish to do larger projects such as the top of a table or a game board. To make a chessboard, cut four strips of light and four strips of dark veneer (Fig. 8); tape together. Then cut into eight pieces and reverse alternate strips (Fig. 9) for checkerboard squares. Glue on, using veneer adhesive. Finish around edges with veneer and decorative inlay strips (Fig. 10), mitered at the corners. An old table can thus become an elegant piece.

Balsa Core Jewelry

Fine veneer wood and inlay make this jewelry appear elegant, but its core is merely balsa which is much easier to shape than hardwood.

Various jewelry creations can be made of the leftover pieces of veneer and decorative inlay borders from other projects.

Read the preceding projects for sources and methods of cutting and using the veneers. After making the wooden components, add jewelry findings and combine with wooden beads, chains, or leather for contemporary creations.

MATERIALS

¼″ (or 3/16″) thick balsa wood; scrap pieces of veneer and preinlaid borders; white glue; stain (or brown paint); small brush; sandpaper; steel wool; knife; coping saw; awl; weights; wax paper; clip clothespins; varnish or paste wax.

Jewelry findings; screw eyes (3/8″ or 7/16″), jump rings; eye pins; chains or beads (see suppliers in Chapter 7); small pliers for assembling jewelry.

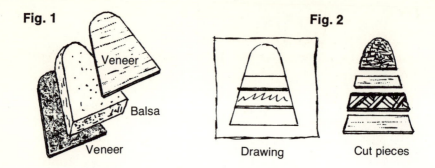

Fig. 1

Veneer

Balsa

Veneer

Fig. 2

Drawing

Cut pieces

The balsa will be sandwiched between veneers (Fig. 1). Veneers can be inlaid (butted against each other), or a single piece of veneer can be overlaid with contrasting shapes, such as the butterfly in the photograph.

Decide on jewelry shapes possible from the veneer pieces you have available. The veneer strips from the hardware store could also be used. Combine veneers with decorative preinlaid borders (see Suppliers; Constantine, Chapter 7). These 36″ borders can be ordered cut in 12″ lengths. Widths vary according to pattern chosen.

On paper, draw an area incorporating inlay border or contrasting veneers. Draw areas to fit veneer around inlay (Fig. 2). See Fig. 9 also for various ideas. For front, cut veneer and inlay to size planned. Cut a piece of balsa wood slightly larger than overall area planned. Cut a veneer piece for back about size of balsa.

Glue front units to one side of balsa. Lay wax paper over and lay on weight or hold with clip clothespins. When glue dries, glue veneer on the back. When the three layers are firmly glued together, trim even with edge of front veneer (Fig. 3), using a knife or coping saw with a fine blade. If added overlay designs are planned, glue these in position now. When all glue is dry, sand piece, using a fine sandpaper.

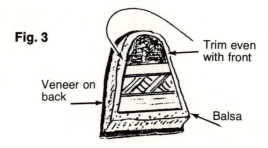

Fig. 3

Trim even with front

Veneer on back

Balsa

Fig. 4   **Fig. 5**

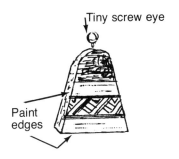

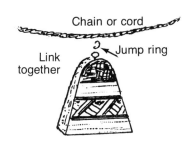

Generally, the balsa color showing at sides is too light unless top is a blond wood. If necessary, darken the balsa with diluted burnt umber acrylic paint or a wood stain. Go over exposed balsa areas with a small brush, being careful not to get color on veneers.

When dry, varnish (or finish piece with paste wax). Spray varnish is handy. Place wood piece in a box or protected area. Spray surface, then turn spray can upside down and spray sides of units until spray stops. Ths clears the spray hole while covering edges. Several coats will be needed to get a good finish for jewelry. After varnish dries, go over surface lightly with steel wool. The smoother the finish, the more quality to the jewelry.

Assemble into jewelry using jewelry findings (see Chapter 7 for descriptions and methods). Insert tiny jewelry screw eyes into the balsa wood core (Fig. 4). Start hole with awl if necessary. Add a bit of glue as screw is inserted to make sure it won't pull out.

After glue is dry, attach to chain, cord, or neck ring by sliding jump ring (Fig. 5) through the screw eye. Beads can be attached using eye pins (Fig. 6). To attach a cord (or thong) to a link, make a loop, slide on a large-hole bead, and bend cord back (Fig. 7). Add glue to the tip of the cord and push in to hole of bead, leaving a small loop at end. When glue is dry, use a large jump link to join cord loop and screw eye (Fig. 8).

Fig. 6   **Fig. 7**   **Fig. 8**

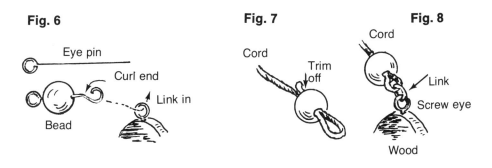

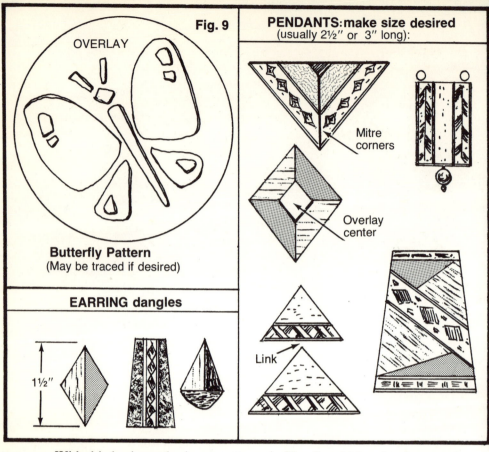

Fig. 9

OVERLAY

Butterfly Pattern
(May be traced if desired)

EARRING dangles

1½"

PENDANTS:make size desired
(usually 2½" or 3" long):

Mitre
corners

Overlay
center

Link

With this basic method, use patterns in Fig. 9 and ideas in photograph to create your own jewelry. Adapt wood you have available; create your own designs.

When making earring drops or any small piece, the ¼" core is too bulky. Before gluing, sand the balsa core, making it about ⅛" thick at top of each piece (Fig. 10). Then glue on the veneers and trim. (Some pendants could be thinner at top also.) To assemble earrings, glue a bell cap (Fig. 11)

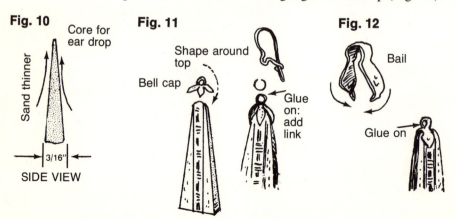

Fig. 10

Core for
ear drop

Sand thinner

3/16"

SIDE VIEW

Fig. 11

Shape around
top

Bell cap

Glue
on:
add
link

Fig. 12

Bail

Glue on

on top of each wood piece. Attach to earring with jump ring. Or use a jewelry finding called a bail (Fig 12). Prongs on each side can be pushed into the wood. To secure, add glue as prongs are inserted.

For the square rods shown in the photo, glue together two pieces of balsa to make thickness equal to the width of a preinlaid border to be used (Fig. 13). Cut, making a square balsa piece just large enough to glue a border piece to each of the four sides. Glue together. Attach screw eyes on both ends. With jump links, add wooden bead or chain tassel (from old jewelry) at end. Attach to a leather or macrame cord and tie around neck (Fig. 14). Or make long enough to tie on for a belt.

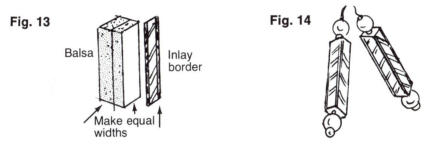

Fig. 13

Balsa

Inlay border

Make equal widths

Fig. 14

With the vast variety of jewelry findings available and these methods of attaching them into the soft balsa core, all kinds of jewelry can be designed. Try sewing elastic through the core to make a bracelet (Fig. 15). To inlay tumbled stones, abalone, or shells, trace shape of object on top veneer, and cut opening. Cut and glue three layers together. Then cut down into the balsa to accommodate the contours of the stone or shell (Fig. 16). Glue in.

Observe current jewelry styles; they change constantly. Adapt this method to create new-fashioned pieces.

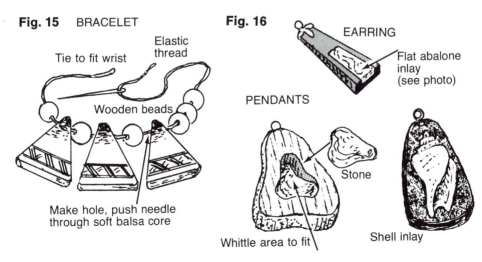

Fig. 15   BRACELET

Tie to fit wrist

Elastic thread

Wooden beads

Make hole, push needle through soft balsa core

Fig. 16

EARRING

Flat abalone inlay (see photo)

PENDANTS

Stone

Whittle area to fit

Shell inlay

Straw Marquetry Box

The entire surface of this box was covered with straw pieces.

The natural sheen of straw makes it a durable, decorative covering. Patterns can be created by alternating direction of strips. Try a traditional box, then an arrangement of your own.

MATERIALS

Straw (wheat or rye); box, old or new; black paint (spray-on or brush-on); black construction paper; white pencil; red or green food coloring (optional).

White glue; wax paper; X-acto knife and scissors.

If you have access to the open country, gather straw any time from early summer to late fall. Allow to dry thoroughly. Most country stores carry straw that is usually well dried and flattened. In the city, around the Christmas holidays, straw can often be purchased for manger scenes. Florists have wheat stalks, but this is an expensive source. Or buy straw by mail (see Chapter 7).

Sort your straw. Note its structure (Fig. 1). Break at each joint and remove outer husks. These are generally too thin to use. Try splitting straw lengthwise; get the feel of it. Some is very brittle; some may need flattening and cleaning. If it is too rigid or brittle, place in a pan, pour boiling water over; and soak overnight.

Straw has a hard, shiny surface that is difficult to dye, but color changes make good accents. Place some pieces of straw in a pan, add food coloring or dye and a little boiling water. Let soak until the water practically evaporates.

Remove all hardware from box and set aside. Paint the box black. Each straw piece can be applied separately, but it is easier and texture variations

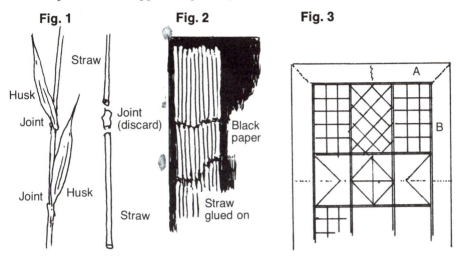

Fig. 1

Straw

Husk

Joint

Joint

Husk

Joint

Straw

Fig. 2

Joint (discard)

Black paper

Straw glued on

Straw

Fig. 3

A

B

can be controlled better by making groupings of narrow strips on black paper. Then cut the paper shapes and apply to the box to create the design.

With a knife or thumbnail, split straw into strips of various widths up to about ⅛″ wide. Spread glue on the black paper and lay strips in place (Fig. 2). The wetness of the glue helps soften and flatten the strips. Keep pressing down, squeezing out any excess glue (it can be removed from the surface later). Lay a piece of wax paper over and place under a weight.

Straw is most effective in simple geometric designs. Plan a design for the box such as the one shown (Fig. 3). Draw checkerboard areas on the box with white pencil. Make a paper pattern of any areas with angles. Corners should miter. Mark a few lines to indicate direction of straw strips which create the texture. Cut each shape out of the straw strips glued onto the black paper (Fig. 4, A and B, for example).

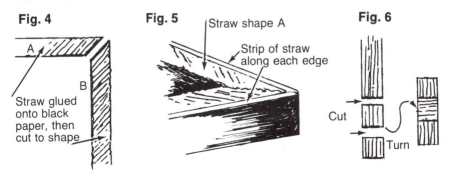

Fig. 4

A

B

Straw glued onto black paper, then cut to shape

Fig. 5

Straw shape A

Strip of straw along each edge

Fig. 6

Cut

Turn

Glue pieces to box, placing shapes near outside edge of box first. Glue a single strip of a straw (Fig. 5) along edge to hide any irregularities and to finish the edge.

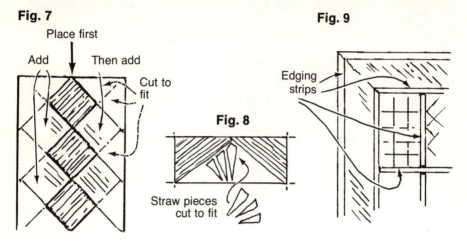

Fig. 7

Place first

Add   Then add

Cut to fit

Fig. 8

Straw pieces cut to fit

Fig. 9

Edging strips

For checkerboard, cut panels about ¼″ wide of the straw strips glued on the black. Then cut across, making squares. alternate direction of straw (Fig. 6). Diamonds are made in similar manner. Cut squares, place center units first, add side ones, and trim as needed to fit (Fig. 7).

Continue cutting areas needed from the black paper with the glued-on straw. Keep preparing more as needed. Glue designs in position on the box. For certain accents (if desired), cut and shape straw pieces to make designs (Fig. 8). Glue a strip of straw along each edge and where pattern areas meet to complete design (Fig 9). Cover sides of box in same manner, using triangles and other geometric shapes (Fig. 10) in any pattern you choose.

When box is completely covered and glue is dry, take a damp cloth and clean off any glue that may be left on the surface.

For the top inner edges of the box and cover, use thinner strips of straw or husks (Fig. 11). It should not add bulk that might prevent closing. Make a lining for the box as described for the Renaissance Jewel box in Chapter 1. Replace hardware.

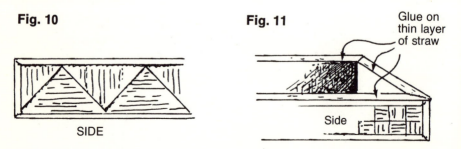

Fig. 10

SIDE

Fig. 11

Glue on thin layer of straw

Side

Straw Work Plaque

Straw lends itself to natural designs. A roughly painted deep brown background enhances the pale sheen of the natural straw on this plaque.

The plaque shown in the photo has a contemporary look. It could be a calendar as shown. Or you might glue into that area a picture, a mirror, or favorite poem. Or make a decorative plaque by placing design nearer the center.

MATERIALS

Wood plaque or piece of masonite 9″ x 13″ (or size desired); dark brown or black paint; other materials same as for straw box.

Paint plaque. On paper, draw a design suitable for plaque such as grasses with a bird, butterfly, kite, or flowers (Fig. 1). Plan a checkerboard edging if desired. With white pencil, redraw design on plaque.

Glue straw on black paper as described for straw box. Make areas of the design, cutting shapes out of the straw glued to the black paper. Glue pieces in place. More casual effects, such as the grasses, can be glued a piece at a time directly to the board. Soak straw, if necessary, to make more pliable. Use knife to trim and shape straw as it is placed.

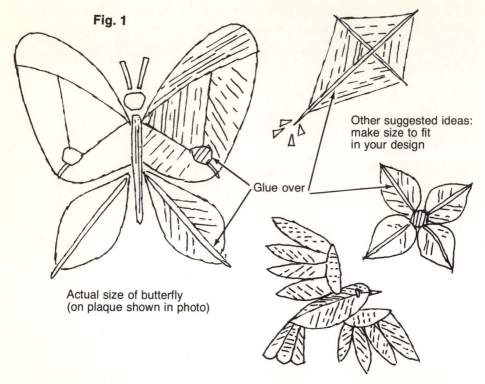

Fig. 1

Actual size of butterfly
(on plaque shown in photo)

Glue over

Other suggested ideas:
make size to fit
in your design

Glue strips along the edges, changing direction at joinings (Fig. 2). Cover raw side edges of board with straw also, if using masonite or plywood.

When complete, allow glue to dry thoroughly, and clean surface with damp rag. Glue in calendar, picture, or whatever you have planned. Attach a hanger in back.

Fig. 2

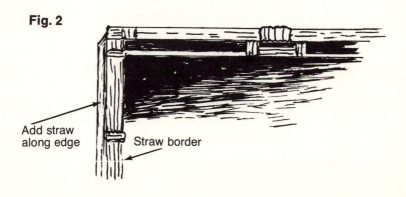

Add straw
along edge

Straw border

5

PAPER

The development of paper was closely related to the development of art and knowledge. In 1200, few people could read or write. At that time, in Italy, possibly because of the large numbers of people who were part of the Church, there was somewhat more literacy than in the rest of Europe. All books had to be tediously copied by hand on parchment (treated animal skin). Most books were copied by monks for the Church. To produce books in quantity, several factors had to come together: letters in movable form, presses, ink, and paper.

The Chinese had learned to make paper around 100 A.D., and the knowledge gradually spread through the Near East with the capture of Oriental craftsmen by Arabs at Samarkand in 751. Arab conquests of Europe spread this knowledge further, and Arabs started paper mills in Spain in the twelfth century. The first papermaking by Europeans was in a mill set up in Fabrino, Italy, around 1276.

Books and Printing:

For some time, artists had known how to obtain prints by cutting designs into a block of wood and transferring the design to fabric. Presses, adapted from ancient wine presses, were improved for this purpose. Religious as well as playing cards were printed from blocks. Also, by the fifteenth

This woodcut (Venice 1499) shows scribes writing books.

A buratto pattern for making a unicorn design, from a book of patterns by the Venetian designer Federico Vinciolo. This book, first published in Turin in 1587, has been copied and translated many times.

century some books were printed, each page carved of a single block of wood, including letters and words. Although more copies could be made, the method was still not practical for making books.

Craftsmen who made armor and those who decorated leather used individual letter stamps to create names and symbols. Metal letters were more durable, but inks of the time would not adhere to metal. Around the fifteenth century, the great artists developed oil painting methods, and from this oil-base color, printing ink was created.

All the elements were now available. In 1455, Gutenberg, in Germany, put them together, placing separate movable type pieces into a frame and printing from it. Thus the printing industry began.

By 1467, books were being published in Italy. Publishing spread rapidly, and knowledge became more readily available, not only to scholars and churchmen, but to merchants, soldiers—all classes, including the craftsmen. Now books made it possible to learn trades or new patterns to make which previously could only be taught in apprenticeship. In Milan in 1522, Alciat published a book on *Emblems,* showing designs for woodcarvers and metalworkers. In 1520 and 1530, the first book of lace pattern designs was published in Italy. In 1532, Vavassore did a book on cross stitch and drawnwork. Other such books followed, which were much in demand throughout Europe.

Ornamental painting on furniture by famous artists was a popular style in the sixteenth century. Books of designs by known artists helped less talented artists produce better work. Later, printed paper designs were used on the furniture and a new craft developed.

Art Povero:

The art of lacquerware had been brought from China and by 1600 was very fashionable in Italy. Skilled craftsmen attempted to recreate the lacquer surfaces of the Oriental pieces. The artist painted designs, and shellac or

This eighteenth century Venetian secretary desk is an elaborate example of Art Povero. For the most part, decorations were made of intricately cut colored engravings, applied to a painted wood surface. The designs on the middle drawers show Chinese influence.

varnishes were used to make the elegant surface. When the motifs were Oriental, the work was called *Chinoiserie*.

To increase production, the master artist had his designs reproduced and printed on paper. The apprentices colored and cut out these prints. After gluing the cutouts to the furniture, the layers of lacquer were added. This production method was scorned and labeled ''Art Povero'' (poor man's art) or *Lacche Povero*.

Gradually it become accepted, and in time art povero became a popular art with the ladies. As a greater selection of prints became available, many of the elite dabbled in this craft. By the eighteenth century, not only furniture, but also boxes, cases, trays, mirror frames, candlesticks, musical instruments, and other objects were decorated in this manner. The technique spread from Italy throughout Europe. In France it was known as decoupage—a more familiar name for this craft.

Religious Cards, Paper Filigree, and Greeting Cards:

Even before Gutenberg printed his first Bible, religious cards printed from wood blocks were distributed by the Church to the faithful. These religious mementos were treasured. In the stark cells of nuns and monks, a single religious card might have been the only ornament. There was a general desire to embellish a card that had been sent by the Pope with whatever means they could find. Yet a humble nun had no funds. In those times, churches were lavished with elaborate gold and silver filigree as well as the finest crafts and art of the country. Sometime around the beginning of the Renaissance, possibly in some Italian cloister, someone discovered the method of making paper filigree. Ornamentation was created by curling narrow paper strips, the trimmings of scrolls or books. The effect was almost as attractive as the precious metal filigrees.

Religious cards were given to the lay people also for special occasions. As printing developed, it was possible to produce more, to satisfy the needs of the general population. These cherished cards were generally set up near a shrine or religious figure in the home.

By the early 1900's, when greeting cards for various occasions were received, these too were added to the religious cards in the home. Certainly, few were ever thrown away. Thus greeting cards became a basis for a charming home craft for the thrifty who wish to keep the colorful cards. The second project in this chapter will show you the method.

Quick Trick Art Povero

These small objects have been decorated with Art Povero. For center plaque, designs were applied to a small piece of red cardboard, which was then edged with gold cord and mounted on another piece of cardboard covered with blue felt. The wood plaque and pendant were painted black. Pearlized nail polish over a silver metal box is the background for the Leo zodiac box; the other box has a white background.

The real fascination that comes of this craft is the selection and artistic arrangement of many delicately cut pieces. It's not just pasting a picture on a board.

To get the feel of the craft, try a small piece with substitute materials. Then if you wish to do real art povero, craft suppliers carry all the special materials needed.

MATERIALS

Small box or plaque or a piece of card (about 3″ x 4″); selection of small prints; small scissors; clear nail polish; enamel paint and brush (or colored nail polish); nail polish remover; soft cloth or rag; white glue; sandpaper (if needed).

Select the small object you wish to decorate: wood, rigid plastic, or metal such as the typewriter ribbon box shown. Sand off any wording and paint a color background with enamel or nail polish.

Select appropriate-size prints for pieces to cut and arrange. Find motifs in magazines, cards, catalogs, calendars, or use prints from books for this purpose (see Dover, Chapter 7).

Plan arrangement and how the prints will be cut for best effects. Try to combine elements with the same sort of line and feeling to make a more integrated decoration. Changing and adapting is part of the creative and exciting part of this craft. Organizing the design shows your artistic talents.

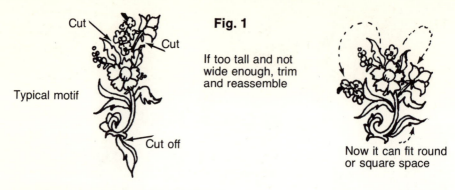

Fig. 1

Cut

Cut

Typical motif

If too tall and not
wide enough, trim
and reassemble

Cut off

Now it can fit round
or square space

Sometimes a flower grouping may be too tall for the space. Cut some blossoms or leaves separately and rearrange to fit (Fig. 1). Frames and borders can also be reassembled. The edge design on the round cupid box was made from two small frames by cutting at logical junctions (Fig. 2). The swag on the top of the black plaque was made from a Christmas wreath print (Fig. 3).

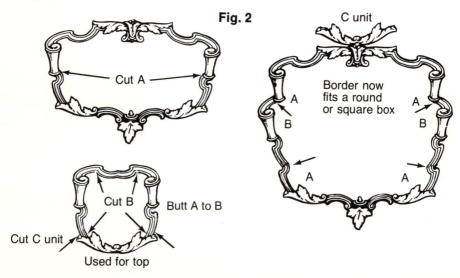

Fig. 2

C unit

Cut A

Border now
fits a round
or square box

A

B

A

B

A

A

Cut B

Butt A to B

Cut C unit

Used for top

After deciding what to use, cut out general areas, leaving a little paper around each. Paint clear nail polish over face of pictures, covering only area to be used. Don't brush back and forth, just lay it on.

Try to avoid pictures with printing on back that might show through on front when glued down. If it is necessary to use some, after nail polish is dry, turn over. Dampen a rag with a little vinegar and rub gently over the back until unwanted printing is removed.

To cut: keep the scissors under the paper so you can see where you are going (Fig. 4). This may seem awkward at first, but soon you'll find it is

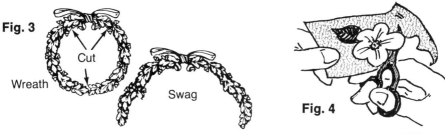

Fig. 3

Wreath

Cut

Swag

Fig. 4

easier to control fine cutting. Place cut pieces in position as you work. When the arrangement is cut, remove pieces and lay to one side.

Take a clean cloth, wet, then wring it out thoroughly. Place at one side. Using a slightly thinned white glue, rub it around on the surface of the object until it makes an even film with no bubbles. Add more water or glue if necessary to get this even film. (If, after the prints are in place, the edges curl, glue was too thin.)

Clean and dry hands, then gently drop units in place in the glue film. Slide them around until each position is satisfactory. Now lay the damp cloth flat over entire surface. Pat down, pressing the paper pieces into the glue. At the same time the damp cloth removes glue from the uncovered areas. Carefully remove cloth when all units are pressed down and properly adhere to the surface. Make sure there are no bubbles or lumps.

Allow glue to set a couple of hours. Again wring out cloth; it should be just slightly damp. Dry hands. Go over surface removing any remaining glue and making sure every tiny edge is glued down. Add glue on any loose edge; press down and clean.

Allow glue to dry a few more hours; again go over cutouts, pressing along edges with a tool such as a nut pick. This thins and blends paper into surface slightly.

Allow glue to dry several days. Then apply a coat of clear nail polish. Allow to dry and apply another coat. When dry, dampen a rag with nail polish remover and rub around over the surface, smoothing as much as possible. Use nail polish and remover in a well-ventilated room. Add another coat of clear nail polish and repeat process several times so thickness of glued-on paper is not as apparent. Finish with a final rubbing of remover to slightly dull the surface.

This method does not give as smooth a surface or ''sink'' the print as much as real art povero, where the prints will appear to become part of the background. To do it properly, prints should be sprayed with a special coating, then cut and glued as described. Then they should be covered with varnish, following instructions on the can. Usually twenty coats of varnish are recommended to get the proper effect. Most craft stores carry decoupage materials. Art povero is a highly skilled craft, worth the effort when you see the smooth, mellow surface of a piece well finished.

Card
Creations

Birthday, anniversary and Mother's Day cards in predominately pink, lavender and soft green colors were selected to make this note holder. For Christmas, use colorful greeting cards, such as shiny foils, to make an elegant card holder.

In many a peasant home, hanging on the wall, yellowed with age, is an aggregation of cherished cards, crocheted or buttonhole-stitched together. In this country, people often ask what can be done with the vast amounts of discarded Christmas cards. Here is an interesting solution, a colorful item to sell at bazaars or give as a gift. Greeting cards for other occasions can be assembled as a remembrance of an occasion. Once you know the procedure, various other shapes can be created: boxes, balls, or arch-shaped units. Just plan length of each edge to match the adjacent edge.

MATERIALS
Assortment of cards (Christmas, birthday, or other special-occasion cards); colored crochet cotton (or embroidery floss), medium thickness; large-holed sturdy needle.

Sort through your collection of cards and select those you wish to use. Select cards for design, shape, subject material, and color scheme. The more carefully the cards are planned, the more attractive the finished unit. Choose horizontal and vertical cards as suggested in Fig. 1. The most interesting and attractive cards should be chosen for positions 1, 2, and 3; and for lower unit 9, 10, and 11.

Cards for positions 1 and 3 should be similar in size, content, and color to complement card 2. This is also true of cards 9 and 11, to fit either side of 10, which can be longer if desired. The cards for the front of the pocket (6, a, b, c) should be horizontal.

As shown, all cards need to add up to about the same width except for the two small cards for sides of the pocket. Make any combination you

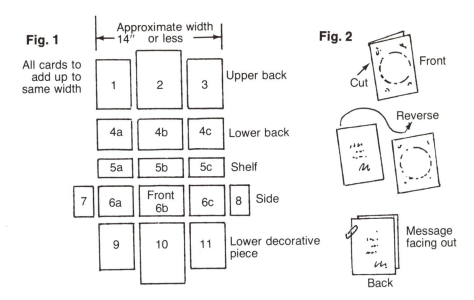

Fig. 1

All cards to add up to same width

Approximate width 14″ or less

1	2	3	Upper back
4a	4b	4c	Lower back
5a	5b	5c	Shelf
7	6a	Front 6b	6c	8	Side
9	10	11	Lower decorative piece

Fig. 2

Front

Cut

Reverse

Message facing out

Back

prefer. Cards for rows 4, 5, or 6 could be two instead of three, as long as the total width matches. Lay out cards selected and determine width you will use. Cards 4 and 5 need not be as attractive as they will not be seen as much. If necessary cut sections from larger cards to fit height and width needed for these.

The height of 7 and 8 (pocket sides) should match height of cards 6a and 6c; the width should be the same as that of 5, the pocket shelf (see Fig. 1). Make some sort of notation on paper where each card is planned to fit.

Both front and back of the card should be used. Cut at fold (Fig. 2) and turn the greeting to the outside. Clip the cards together.

Thread the needle with crochet cotton. To edge, use buttonhole stitch (see Chapter 7 Stitchery). Hold the front and back firmly together and push the needle in through both cards at regular intervals about ¼″ in from the edge (Fig. 3). Holes should be about ¼″ apart. You can measure and mark these holes on the card. Or space by eye as you sew. Go through each hole

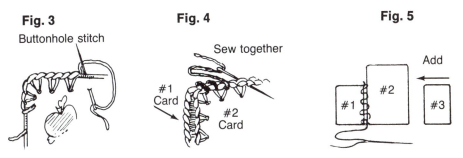

Fig. 3

Buttonhole stitch

Fig. 4

Sew together

#1 Card

#2 Card

Fig. 5

Add

#1 #2 #3

twice, making two buttonhole stitches. When completely around card, tie thread, pull between cards, and cut off. Go around another card in the same manner, sewing the front to the back. Continue until all cards are edged with the buttonhole stitching.

Then assemble the unit. Sew side of card 1 to side of card 2. Run the threaded needle between stitching, catching top of buttonhole stitch on alternate card edges (Fig. 4). This holds the two cards together. Pull up just enough so cards lay flat side by side (Fig. 5). Continue sewing cards to each other in the same manner, attaching to make each of the five rows shown in Fig. 1.

Then assemble: sew first and second rows together; add shelf. Next add 7 and 8, pocket sides (Fig. 6). Add the bottom row by folding up shelf (pocket base) and attaching unit (9, 10, 11) to same edge as shelf (Fig. 7).

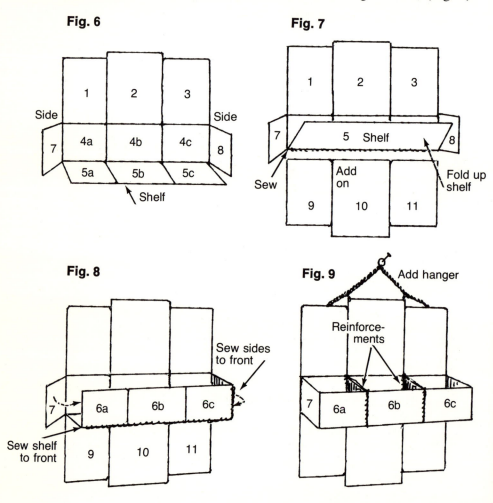

Fig. 6

Fig. 7

Fig. 8

Fig. 9

Front of pocket, row 6, a, b, c, is sewn on last (Fig. 8).

If cards used are large, the pocket may droop. Cut two cards the height of pocket, width of shelf. Edge as before and sew into joinings before attaching front of pocket (Fig. 9).

The joinings are flexible, and many shapes and combinations are possible. Make an arrangement that shows off your most attractive cards. It is advisable to keep the overall width under 15".

Braid a cord, attach to top (Fig. 9) and hang up this creation of cards. For the holidays, it can hold new greeting cards as they arrive, or for all year, use it to hold general notes and other trivia.

Paper Filigree

Two examples of quillwork. On the right a floral group was placed in a small oval frame. On the left, a Christmas card picture was glued onto a piece of black cardboard, then colored quillwork was glued around it.

Neglected since the eighteenth century, this craft is again popular and is now known as quilling. Learn a few basics and then embellish a favorite photograph or make a quillwork design to frame.

MATERIALS

Paper strips ⅛" wide (cut your own or obtain from a craft supply); hatpin; toothpick; corsage pins (or straight pins); white glue (that dries clear).

Wax paper; piece of corrugated cardboard about 8" x 10"; masking tape; plaque and photo (or whatever you wish to ornament); paint, paper, or fabric (for background); clear acrylic spray (optional).

Decide what you would like to enhance with paper filigree. Select a small photo, a print, a favorite saying or poem. Cut a backing of cardboard or wood at least 2″ larger than photo or print—about 4″ x 5″ is good. Or use a picture frame if there is ⅛″ depth behind the glass. Some frames have bulky cardboard in back that can be removed to allow depth. For wood backing, use natural color or paint it. If using cardboard backing, cover with plain dark-colored fabric or paper.

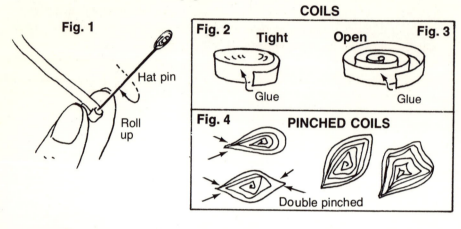

Before making a design, practice a few of the basic quillwork shapes. Cut a strip of the ⅛″-wide paper about 4″ long. Hold in left hand, hatpin (or toothpick) in right. Press hatpin into end of strip (or dampen if necessary) to start strip curling. Now roll the paper strip around hatpin, maintaining tension with left hand (Fig. 1). When strip is rolled up, remove pin. With toothpick, add a dab of glue to end and hold until set. This forms a tight roll for accents or flower centers (Fig. 2). Roll another strip, then gently release tension and let it uncoil slightly (Fig. 3). Add glue to end to prevent opening further. The openness can be varied.

These basic open coils can be altered by pinching in at various spots. Try pinching a loose coil on one side, another at two sides, and you will see the possibilities (Fig. 4).

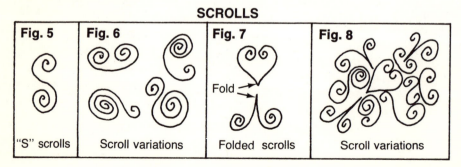

Scrolls are not glued. Cut a strip about 2″ long, curl one end, turn around, and curl other end (Fig. 5). Paper will hold its curl. When shapes are glued to each other and onto a surface, the size and sweep of the curve can be controlled. Try variations of the basic scroll. Roll in from both sides, curl more to one side (Fig. 6).

Pinch the strip once before curling (Fig. 7) to create the heart or V-shape. Try many variations. Lay these practice pieces next to each other, shifting them about (Fig. 8). You'll find they create interesting designs.

Now that you know the basics, you can create a design of your own or use a pattern. To frame a photo as shown and place flowers at the side, trace the pattern (Fig. 9) on paper. Tape a piece of wax paper around the corrugated cardboard (Fig. 10). Slide the paper pattern under the wax paper. Cut

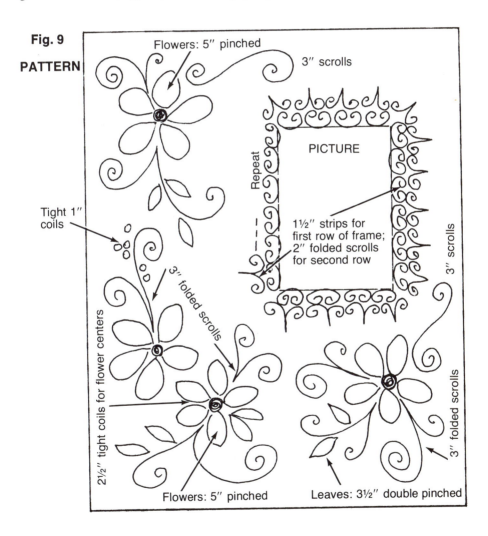

Fig. 9

PATTERN

Flowers: 5″ pinched

3″ scrolls

Repeat

PICTURE

1½″ strips for first row of frame; 2″ folded scrolls for second row

Tight 1″ coils

3″ folded scrolls

2½″ tight coils for flower centers

3″ scrolls

3″ folded scrolls

Flowers: 5″ pinched

Leaves: 3½″ double pinched

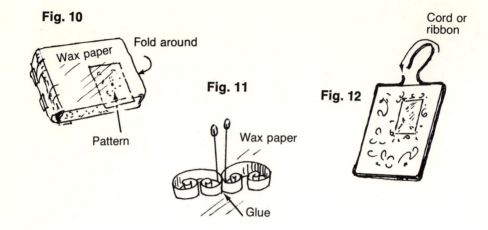

Fig. 10

Wax paper

Fold around

Pattern

Fig. 11

Wax paper

Glue

Cord or ribbon

Fig. 12

strips of paper length indicated on the pattern. Curl shapes as shown. Lay curled pieces on the wax paper over the pattern. Place a glob of glue at corner of board on wax paper. Dip into it as needed. With a toothpick, apply glue at each adjacent point. It takes only the tiniest dab to hold the delicate paper.

Stick pins vertically in the board on either side of each glued point to help hold it together until glue sets (Fig. 11). When glue is dry, lift design off the wax paper. It is quite sturdy once assembled. Glue the picture to your backing board. Add small dabs of glue at base of curled strips where they will attach to board, lay filigree border around the picture, and gently press in position. Glue flower motifs in place.

If desired, lightly spray with clear acrylic to add luster and help preserve the paper curls. A print can be sprayed, but a photo should be masked before spraying.

Glue a velvet ribbon or cord along the edges of card and make a hanging loop by gluing ends (Fig. 12). Or completed piece can be placed in a frame.

The design shown can be adapted to edge any small picture as the border is a repeat. It can use less or more units as needed. Stretch or tighten scrolls slightly to make them come out even at corners. Add more or vary flower shapes and curves of tendrils for larger areas. A few flowers and a scroll edging around an invitation or announcement is a popular use of quilling.

Or flowers can be clustered to make an arrangement with no photo, as shown in photograph on page 111.

6

COMBINED MATERIALS: TOYS AND CELEBRATIONS

I n Italy, as in the rest of the world, for centuries long working hours were relieved by celebrations and amusements. From the Middle Ages to the present, most all observances were centered around religious holidays. Festivals, parades, and church attendance were a vital part of life in Italy.

Parents made toys for their children, carved or stuffed dolls, whittled wooden toys. Often such toys had simple motions, such as pecking birds or jumping-jack toys, animated by a string.

When a traveling entertainment group arrived in a small town, everyone would take time out. Some groups presented circus-type acts, others puppet shows.

Puppetry in Italy:

Jointed figurines moved by the will of an operator are very ancient; probably they were used in pagan rituals for magic effects. Commoners would be awed by moving statues. It is believed marionettes (manipulated by strings) and rod puppets go back to Roman times.

Some puppetry was used in the Middle Ages to depict Biblical scenes. Later, secular shows were popular, and the Church scorned puppetry as

This old woodcut (sixteenth century) shows a puppet-maker at work.

idolatry. The comic exaggerated character was revived from Roman times. By the sixteenth century, this type of show spread throughout Europe. An Italian puppet of the time is believed to be part of the origin of the now familiar Punch and Judy. Punchinello was originally a large stringed marionette. Gradually it evolved into the hand puppet, Punch.

A Renaissance poet, Ariosto, elaborating on an old legend, wrote "Orlando Furioso," a story of knighthood and chivalry. A special type of marionette developed, dramatizing these tales. Orlando marionettes were most popular in Sicily. There were heroes to cheer, villains to hiss, and much violent action on the stage.

A puppeteer, by manipulation of the strings and arm rod, can make this Orlando type puppet duel, draw, or sheath his sword. The visor can be closed by means of a string near the head rod.

Two Orlando puppets are engaged in battle on stage with backdrops. These puppets are large; notice the scale of the wide floorboards.

Manipulated by a rigid rod attached to the neck and back, these puppets were huge, some as tall as four feet and weighing up to eighty pounds. A rod controlled the right arm and other motions were controlled by strings. The knights had armor and shields of embossed and decorated metal. A string through a hole in the right hand was attached to a sword in the scabbard. Thus the puppet could draw his sword and fight noisy, gory battles. Heads appeared to be severed by unhooking from the neck at a strategic moment. These puppet plays, "Orlando Furioso," were continuing dramas of intrigue, magic, loves, and battles.

Holidays and Occasions:

Festivals and holidays varied, each town having its festival day in honor of a special saint or historical occasion. Traditional celebrations often go back for many centuries. The saint or Madonna was carried through the town with a reverent procession of churchmen and devout followers. In a small town, a wedding, christening, or communion would be a holiday for the whole town. The weeks preceding Ash Wednesday were celebrated by "Carnevale," often with costumes and huge masks or puppets representing allegorical figures.

A woodcarver of Valgardena making religious figures. On the table near the center is a wood block ready for carving. Figures such as these are often placed in a presepio.

Christmas was celebrated in many ways from Advent to Epiphany. Some of the origins of our present year-end festival may go back to pagan times and the celebration of Saturnalia. It was a time of merrymaking, rejoicing in the rebirth of the sun and the promise of spring to come. It was the time of gift giving, and wax candles, clay dolls, and trinkets were sold in the market to be given as presents.

When Romans became Christians, this time of year became a holy observance. *Natale* means birth in Italian. The devout would go to church for nine nights before Christmas and to midnight mass on Christmas Eve. In some towns the Piferai (bagpipers) came down from the hills and played through the streets.

January 6, Epiphany, is the day to exchange gifts, as it's believed to be the day the wise men arrived (twelve days after Christmas). Another Italian tradition: gifts are brought by an old hag, Befana, to the good children. During the period from Christmas Eve to Epiphany, small statues of the holy family, angels, shepherds, and wise men were set up in churches and in each home. Called the Presepio, this miniature manger is an Italian tradition.

Presepio:

Derived from the Latin word *Praesaepe,* meaning "stable" or "manager," the presepio (plural is presepi) is a re-creation or small replica of the Bethlehem stable where Jesus was born. It has been made in many forms.

Detail of the focal point of a large presepio in a museum in Naples.

The church of Maria Maggiore (built around the fifth century), dedicated to the Virgin and Child, had small figures placed there depicting the nativity around 1291.

Throughout Italy, folk craftsmen as well as those working for the churches made figurines and settings of the event. Made of clay or wood, many were crude representations, sometimes painted. Gradually over the years the figures became increasingly more realistic (although folk artists undoubtedly continued to make their own style).

This section of an old presepio with multitudes of figures, shows the tavern; cheese and other foods hang by the door. Women bring food while people eat and play music. Many people and animals are depicted around the tavern.

By the middle of the seventeenth century, churches in Rome and Naples had elegant scenes of assembled figures. Clothing was made of fabric and laces, and other details were added of gold, silver, and jewels. By the end of the seventeenth century the nobility vied with each other to have the finest presepio in their homes. Skilled artists and sculptors were commissioned, and considerable sums were spent on these presepi, which often occupied a whole room.

In Sicily, figures were carved, clothing made of linen dipped in a type of plaster, shaped, and painted. In Lucca, stucco and plaster figures were originally made in the convents. Later the townspeople made them, often for export.

Most spectacular were the presepi of Naples. Special groupings were commissioned for a church as early as 1478. By the seventeenth century, over 400 churches in Naples had elaborate presepi, as well as smaller ones in most homes. A dominican friar, Gregorio Rocco, urged everyone, even the poor, to make one for their home. For those who would never travel, the presepio enabled them to feel part of the Bethlehem scene.

The wealthy, by the eighteenth century, commissioned special sculptors. Called *figurai,* these men spent their lives creating the magnificent characters for the presepi. Many were specialists. Some did only animals, others made only shepherds or angels, others still life pieces.

The king of Naples at the time, Carlos III, had an intense interest in the presepi. He personally arranged and developed the backgrounds. The queen and her attendants sewed the finery for the figures. Fabrics were especially woven with small-scale patterns.

Neopolitan presepi often showed whole scenes, not just the manager. Clothing was usually of current fashion, the setting a local scene or Roman ruins. Often a tavern was included, showing the activity of everyday life. The lavish Neopolitan presepio created a drama filled with emotion and elegance, reflecting the exuberance of the people and their strong religious feeling.

In this century many Italian homes still have a small traditional presepio. Some craftsmen may yet spend their spare time making new figures each year so that during the Christmas season they can display the presepio for all the townspeople to come and see.

Pinocchio Puppet

This Pinocchio puppet made of dowels and wooden spoons has rigid head and arm rods like the Orlando puppets. Manipulation of the rods and strings makes him perform.

Pinocchio, the story of a puppet who wanted to be a boy, was part of the childhood for several generations of Italians. Collodi wrote this classic in the last century, and since then it has been translated into many languages. It should be reread, no matter what your age. Instructions follow to make a *fantoccino* (a puppet animated by wires). Then you can give a performance of Pinocchio, based on the story. This wooden spoon figure is based on the large Orlando rod puppets.

MATERIALS

Two unfinished wooden spoons (spoon bowl should be about 2½" long); one ⅜"-diameter dowel (usually about 2 feet long at lumberyard or craft store); 3¼" x 2" x ¾" block of wood (pine or any scrap available); 2 wooden beads or small knobs about ½" to ¾" diameter (or acorns this size); two wire coat hangers; 17 screw eyes (holes about ¼" or less), 2 small nails.

White glue (Sobo—for wood and fabric); rough and fine sandpaper; red and orange felt (see patterns for sizes); brown yarn; old sock; 5" piece of bulky, bright-colored yarn; 20" piece of string; black felt-tipped marker; paper for patterns; tape; rubber bands.

Tools: coping saw (jigsaw or any saw available); awl; hand drill (⅛" and ⅜" bits); hammer; wire-cutter pliers; knife.

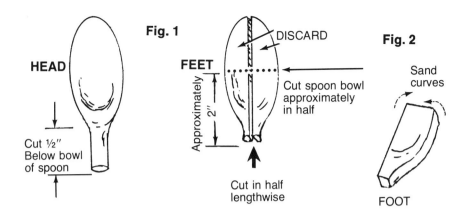

Fig. 1

HEAD

Cut ½"
Below bowl
of spoon

FEET

Approximately 2"

DISCARD

Cut spoon bowl
approximately
in half

Cut in half
lengthwise

Fig. 2

Sand
curves

FOOT

This project does not require a workshop; simple hand tools are adequate. However, a small vise is helpful to hold wood while sawing. The spoon shapes are used so that no curved or shaped cutting is necessary. All sawing will be small, straight cuts.

For head and feet, cut wooden spoons as shown (Fig. 1). Size of spoons may vary, so use judgment in planning proportions. Sand curves at front corners of feet (Fig. 2), and smooth with the fine sandpaper.

Drill four holes in spoon for head, using ⅛" drill (Fig. 3). Bottom hole should not go all the way through. Make a center hole for the nose using ⅜" drill bit (see Fig. 4 for position). For eyes on front of spoon (concave part), position as shown (Fig. 4), about ¾" apart. With a felt-tip marker, color in black dots about 3/16" diameter.

Fig. 3

Fig. 4

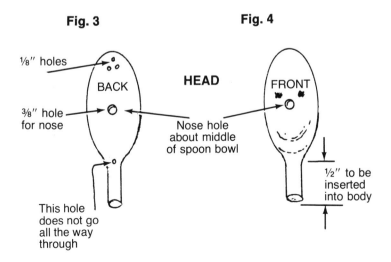

⅛" holes

BACK

⅜" hole
for nose

This hole
does not go
all the way
through

HEAD

Nose hole
about middle
of spoon bowl

FRONT

½" to be
inserted
into body

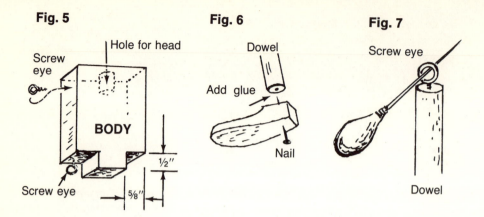

Fig. 5

Screw eye

Hole for head

BODY

½"

⁵⁄₈"

Screw eye

Fig. 6

Dowel

Add glue

Nail

Fig. 7

Screw eye

Dowel

For body, cut wood with leg notches as shown (Fig. 5). Drill a ⅜" hole in center top about ½" deep. Sand body smooth.

Make arms and legs of dowels (or use spoon handles). Cut four pieces 3" long for legs, four pieces 2" long for arms. Smooth ends with sandpaper. With an awl, make a small hole in bottom of one foot piece. Nail through, add glue, and nail into end of one of the 3" dowel pieces (Fig. 6). Repeat for other foot.

To assemble, use awl to make holes in center of end of each dowel. Insert screw eyes in each end. Use awl to help turn it in (Fig. 7). Place a screw eye at each leg notch and each shoulder (see Fig. 5).

To interlock screw eyes, use pliers to twist eye open. Twist sideways, not straight out; then it will be easier to close again (Fig. 8). Open eye just enough to slip in the closed eye of the other piece, then close again. If too

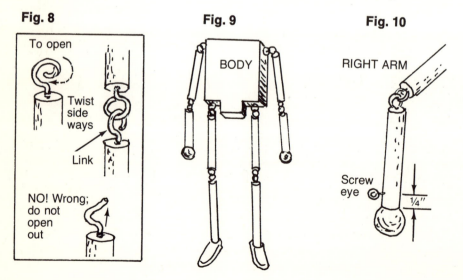

Fig. 8

To open

Twist side ways

Link

NO! Wrong; do not open out

Fig. 9

BODY

Fig. 10

RIGHT ARM

Screw eye

¼"

tight, unscrew slightly, then screw in again. Assemble body (Fig. 9), linking elbows, knees, etc. If feet do not face forward, turn any of the screws slightly until feet set properly. For hands, glue bead (or acorn—sand off tip) at end of each arm. Make hole with awl and add a screw eye about ¼″ from end of dowel of right arm as shown (Fig. 10).

Cut tops off wire coat hangers; discard tops. Cut a body rod about 16″ long. Bend about ⅛″ at one end, making a right angle. Add glue and slide this end into the hole at the base of the head in back (Fig. 11). Cut a piece of brown yarn about 6½″ long, and push through the two drilled holes near top. Add glue and tie around wire (Fig. 11). The wire should now be firmly attached to back of head. Bend top of this wire to fit over your hand (Fig. 12); wind a piece of tape around the rough end.

For puppet's hand wire, straighten wire to make about 20″ long. Use pliers to bend end into a small loop, slip through screw eye on puppet's right wrist, and close loop. Make a ¾″ loop at top of wire and tape rough end (Fig. 12).

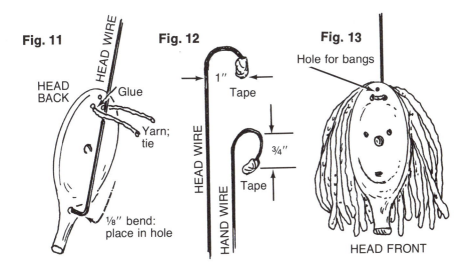

Fig. 11

HEAD WIRE

HEAD BACK

Glue

Yarn; tie

⅛″ bend: place in hole

Fig. 12

HEAD WIRE

1″

Tape

HAND WIRE

¾″

Tape

Fig. 13

Hole for bangs

HEAD FRONT

For hair, cut about 32 strands of brown yarn about 8″ long (depending on your spoon size). Tie in center with a piece of yarn. Add glue over top half of spoon in back. Slip the bunch of yarn in back of spoon between wood and wire (Fig. 13). Arrange yarn and hold with rubber bands until glue dries. For bangs, cut eight strands of yarn about 3½″ long. Tie in center. Add glue just below top edge of spoon. Slip one end of the tie through top center hole; tie on top to secure bangs. Arrange and allow to dry. Top edge of spoon should be exposed to provide a firm surface to glue on hat. Neatly trim ends of yarn above eye level and around the back.

Fig. 14

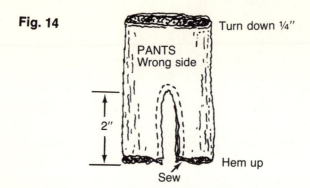

Turn down ¼″

PANTS
Wrong side

2″

Sew

Hem up

For nose, cut a 2″ piece of dowel, whittle to a point on one end. Shape with rough sandpaper, then smooth with fine. Add glue in nose hole, insert dowel end. Add glue in hole in top of body, insert head. Allow to dry and make sure it is firmly attached.

For pants, cut a 4½″ piece of leg part of an old sock (such as brightly colored knee sock). Cut up 2″ in center (Fig. 14). Turn wrong side out and sew up between legs. Turn about ½″ up at bottom of legs and sew. Turn right side out. Fold top under ¼″; run a basting thread around the waist. Add glue about waist level, pull on pants, and fit in place. Pull up basting thread, fitting around the wood; press fabric into glue, making as flat as possible. Hold with rubber bands until dry.

Enlarge hat and vest patterns (Fig. 15) on paper, (see Chapter 7); draw other half of each. Cut hat of orange felt, glue on brim. Add glue on top of head and to the overlap of hat. Fit around on top of head, wire going through peak of hat (Fig. 16). Cut vest of bright-colored felt. Place around figure and glue on top (flat) part of shoulders, overlapping as indicated on pattern. Adjust if necessary to make it set properly. Tie bulky yarn around the neck.

Fig. 15

PATTERN

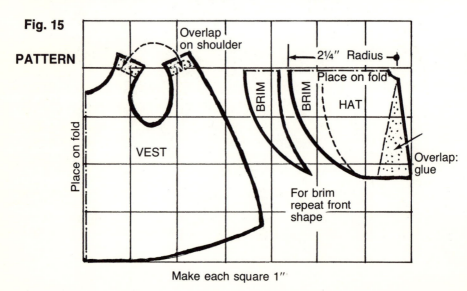

Overlap on shoulder

2¼″ Radius

Place on fold

BRIM

BRIM

HAT

Place on fold

VEST

Overlap: glue

For brim repeat front shape

Make each square 1″

Tie a 20″ piece of string around the left wrist with a small loop in the other end. To manipulate Pinocchio, hold body rod in left hand, slip string loop on little finger. Manipulate his right arm rod with your right hand. Walking is accomplished by turning body rod, swinging and swaying so feet flop into a walk. This puppet is limber and should perform well with a little practice. When not in use, slip arm rod over body rod and hang up. This Orlando type will not tangle as much as the usual string marionettes.

If you enjoyed making this puppet and feel ambitious, create some other characters from the book and give a performance. Wooden shapes can be similar. Paint appropriate features or carve faces of Balsa wood and glue to front of spoon (Fig. 17). Dress appropriately. Length of dowels can be varied to achieve different heights of characters.

An Orlando knight with armor would be a real challenge. Try aluminum cans and pie plates for armor, attach a shield to left arm, and make a hat with a plume. Forget the nose, cut a handsome face from a magazine, and paste face on the spoon bowl.

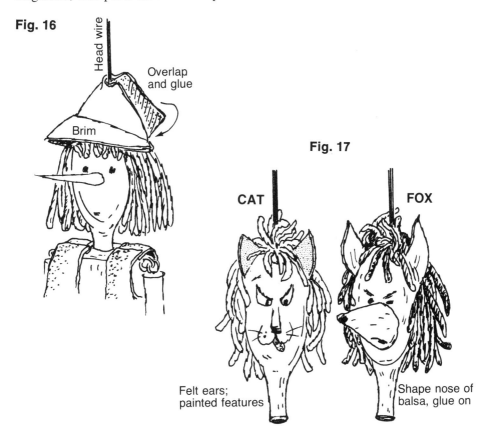

Fig. 16

Head wire

Overlap and glue

Brim

Fig. 17

CAT

FOX

Felt ears; painted features

Shape nose of balsa, glue on

A family treasure to be set up each Christmas season, the presepio shown here was created out of various packing materials. Cherubim and angels fly near papier maché pillars; figurines are clothed in real fabrics. A horse, with newly added trappings, emerges from a shallow arch; fuzzy sheep and a dog add to the feeling of the street scene. The diagram shows the basic units used to make the setting shown. Instructions follow for making your own — a simple one or two level setting or something more complex, as shown.

Presepio: The Setting

The fabric-covered figures and setting shown were inspired by the fabulous seventeenth century presepi. Figurines for nativity groups can usually be purchased around the holiday season. These vary considerably in quality and size. Or you may have accumulated assorted ones over the years and wish to refurbish them and put them into an interesting setting. Their size will determine the scale to make. The setting shown, about 4' high, was made for figures about 8" high. First work on the setting.

MATERIALS

Rigid foam packing corners, blocks of various sizes and shape, plus Styrofoam piece (from craft store), as needed.

Newspaper; wallpaper paste; prepared papier-maché (Celluclay from craft store); latex housepaint; acrylic artist's paint; paintbrushes.

Glue to hold foam (such as Sobo); pegs—⅛" dowels (or skewer sticks, old matchsticks, or other wooden sticks); lightweight cardboard; serrated knife; coping saw or small saw (any serrated edge to cut foam); awl; masking tape.

Optional for columns: ½" to 1" dowels, (depending on size of presepio) or cardboard tubes from gift wrap paper.

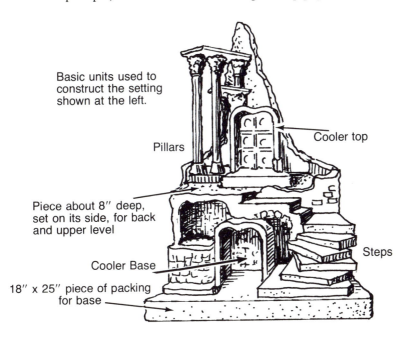

Basic units used to construct the setting shown at the left.

Pillars

Cooler top

Piece about 8" deep, set on its side, for back and upper level

Cooler Base

Steps

18" x 25" piece of packing for base

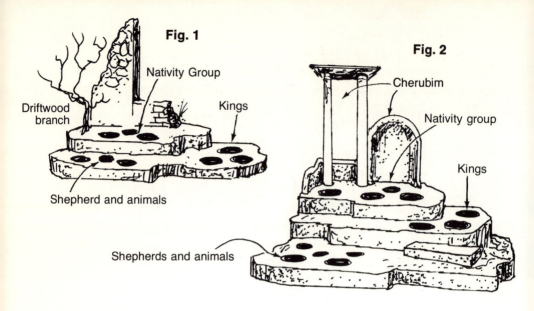

Fig. 1

Nativity Group

Driftwood branch

Kings

Shepherd and animals

Fig. 2

Cherubim

Nativity group

Kings

Shepherds and animals

Have everyone save carton packing corners (the rigid foam, Styrofoam-type material). Gather a large selection. In the one shown, arches were made of a foam six-pack cooler (for summer picnics); base: packing of a stereo set, plus many other odd shapes. Steps were cut from a 1″-thick Styrofoam slab from the craft store.

Gather figures and decide how many levels you will need. Two levels (Fig. 1) are good for five or six figures. Add more levels for larger groupings. Columns and arches can be added to larger pieces (Fig. 2). Visualize your figures and plan an arrangement best suited to them. Make a tracing on paper of base of each figure. As you build, keep checking flat areas to allow room for figures to stand. Consider size and area where you plan to display completed unit and make sure it does not get too large.

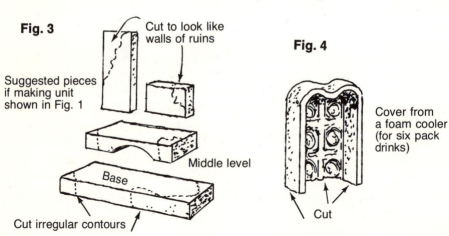

Fig. 3

Cut to look like walls of ruins

Suggested pieces if making unit shown in Fig. 1

Middle level

Base

Cut irregular contours

Fig. 4

Cover from a foam cooler (for six pack drinks)

Cut

Begin piling up the rigid foam shapes like building blocks. Utilize holes and openings if possible; otherwise these can be ignored and covered later. Use largest pieces for base and back (Fig. 3); pile several together as needed. Then add smaller pieces.

When entire piece can generally be visualized, cut foam wherever needed, using a serrated cutting edge. Cutting may produce many tiny static scraps. Although clean, they're messy, so choose an appropriate place to work. Rough edges can be "sanded" by rubbing two cut edges together. Stack as you cut. Tape temporarily to help plan arrangement. Make sure there are large enough level areas for figures to stand.

The three nativity figures should have a dominant position. To make an arch or doorway look with a foam cooler, cut cover to create a flat base (Fig. 4). The cutoff area can be incorporated elsewhere, if desired.

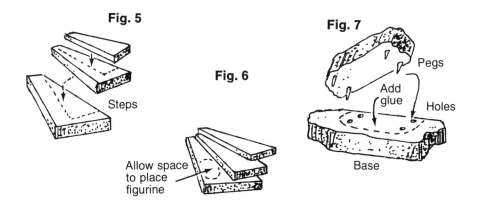

Fig. 5

Fig. 6

Fig. 7

Steps

Allow space to place figurine

Pegs

Add glue

Holes

Base

For steps, cut a wide base piece (Fig. 5); top with smaller angled pieces. Edges need not align. The angles allow more room for figures to stand (Fig. 6). If in doubt about shaping some pieces, it may help to make paper patterns first. Pieces can be butted to make larger units, if necessary.

When gluing, larger pieces will hold better if pegged. Cut ½" (or so) pieces of wooden sticks—anything about ⅛" or ¼" in diameter. Make hole in foam with an awl; add glue to tip of stick and push into piece. Push unit down in area planned to locate position of hole on other piece (Fig. 7). Poke second hole with awl. Spread glue on flat area between the two pieces and in holes. Firmly press pieces together and weight down. Larger pieces could use pegs in each corner. On smaller ones, a peg or two is adequate.

Glue largest units first; when glue dries, add smaller ones. Hold small pieces with masking tape which can be left in place after glue dries. It will be covered later.

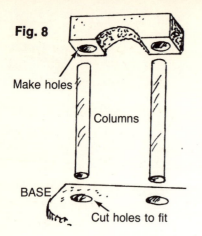

Fig. 8

Make holes

Columns

BASE

Cut holes to fit

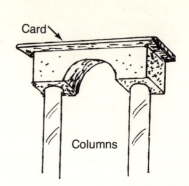

Fig. 9

Card

Columns

If desired, add columns. Measure to determine height in scale with your scene. Cut columns of tubes or dowels. Select a piece of foam packing for top. Some have shapes that add to the effect (Fig. 8). Cut holes into the foam base to fit each column; add glue and insert columns. Cut holes in top piece, add glue, and place unit on top of columns. Cut a piece of cardboard slightly larger than top and glue in position (Fig. 9).

After gluing, entire unit should hold together, yet be light and easy to move. If an undesired opening shows, glue or tape a piece of cardboard over hole. Cover small holes with masking tape.

Tear strips of newspaper about 1″ wide. Dip in a thick solution of wallpaper paste, squeeze out, and lay strips over areas needed so it will no longer look like just a stack of foam shapes. Leave most horizontal flat areas as the original surfaces. Add strips to most intersections of horizontal and vertical surfaces (Fig. 10) over joinings and where pieces were butted together. Also build out over cardboards covering holes and cover masking

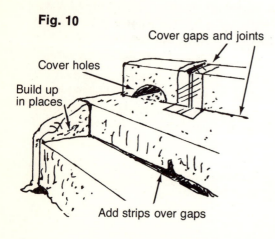

Fig. 10

Cover gaps and joints

Cover holes

Build up
in places

Add strips over gaps

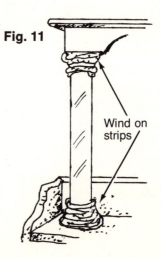

Fig. 11

Wind on
strips

132

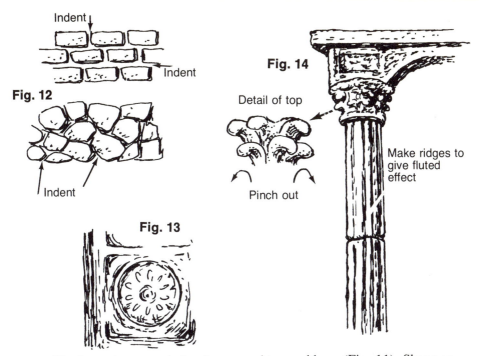

Indent

Fig. 12

Indent

Indent

Fig. 14

Detail of top

Pinch out

Make ridges to give fluted effect

Fig. 13

tapes. If using columns, wind strips around top and base (Fig. 11). Shape as shown. Allow to dry.

To make details and surface textures, mix some prepared papiêr-mache. Cover certain vertical surfaces with ¼″ layer and allow to harden slightly. Then indent with a knife or tool to create the look of stone or old brick (Fig. 12). On other areas, lay on a thin layer of maché, then roughen to look like stucco or rough stone. Place a ¼″ layer in the circles of the arched area cut from cooler. Press in a decorative button, remove to create an effect of a carved door panel (Fig. 13).

On tops of columns, add a generous layer of mache, then pinch out dabs of mache to give effect of decorative carving at top (Fig. 14). Cover columns and base with ¼″ layer. Press in ridges here and there for fluting (Fig. 14). Don't make too even; try to create the effect of old ruins.

When all maché is dry, give entire unit a coat of latex housepaint; any old latex is fine. If several leftover cans are available, mix together; a bumpy grayish or brownish tone makes a good base color.

When paint is dry, color certain areas with acrylic paint. Add a few green areas where sheep will stand or for moss-covered stones. Paint brick textures brownish red; various grays on stone textures. To make more antique-looking, paint a thin solution of burnt umber over an area, then rub off surface.

When dry, set each figure in planned area. Remove and paint the base of each figure to match the color of area where it stands.

133

Presepio Figurines

Commercial painted figures can be used in your completed setting. To get more the feeling of an old Neapolitan presepio, dress figurines in actual fabrics. It enhances the appearance of purchased figures and can refurbish old figures that may be cracked or worn. Larger figures, 6″ to 8″ or more, are easier to handle.

MATERIALS
Presepio figurines and other figures in scale (new or old figures of any material); cherubim from craft store, about 2½″ high (optional).

    Assortment of fabrics—velvets, satin, lining materials, etc.; various narrow cords for edging, such as colored soutache, gold cord, baby rick rack, gift wrap cords.

    Sobo glue; jewels, star and other trims; tissue paper (or discarded dress pattern); wax paper; flesh colored acrylic paint and brush (optional, if needed).

The larger the selection of scraps or fabric available, the richer the final result. Gather scraps and small trims from all sources: garage sales, second-hand shops (an old evening blouse might make a king's garment or angel robe). Collections could be pooled if several families each made this project, or it could be a church project.

Most fabrics should be lightweight to better shape onto the contours. Use elegant fabrics for kings; velvet could be used on cloaks. Select appropriate color, texture, and weight of fabric for each part of each figure. The painted-on colors can be used as a guide, if desired. The existing shaping of the garment will generally have to be followed.

For old figures, touch up faces and hands with paint if they are chipped or dingy. Cherubim (usually sold in sets in the craft stores) generally come all gold. Paint bodies flesh tone, leaving wings and hair gold.

These three kings, which had been in the family for years, had become badly chipped, cracked and worn. By repainting in places and adding velvet cloaks, satin or brocade garments, a fur collar, beads, jewels and gold trims they once again became elegant pieces for the presepio.

To make a pattern, cut a piece of tissue paper, lay around figure, marking area needed. Do undergarment first, then add overgarment, sash, sleeves and finally cloak. Cut out pattern piece and lay on again to check fit. Don't try to do a complete garment in one piece (Fig. 1). Usually back, front and each arm can be made separately, depending on gesture of figure. Avoid too many layers; dressed figures should not look any bulkier than in painted clothes.

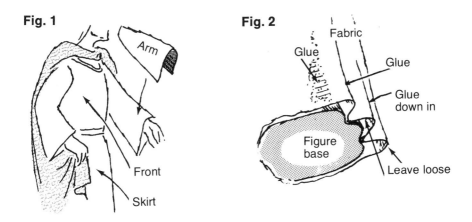

Fig. 1

Arm

Front

Skirt

Fig. 2

Fabric

Glue

Glue

Glue down in

Figure base

Leave loose

Using pattern, cut shape of fabric, allowing a little extra. Add glue to figure; press fabric in place. Butt edges or overlap slightly; trim if needed. Take a small piece of wax paper and lay over fabric so your fingers won't stick. Keep pressing until glue holds and cloth adheres to figures in folds as desired. Some folds can be loose, only gluing into grooves (Fig. 2).

After glue dries, trim edges if necessary. Add a little glue under trimmed edge or overlaps to make sure it holds and does not ravel. Add next layer. Capes can be slightly heavier. If using velvet, turn pattern over and lay on wrong side; cut velvet from back. For more elegance, length of train of cloak can sometimes be longer than on actual figure.

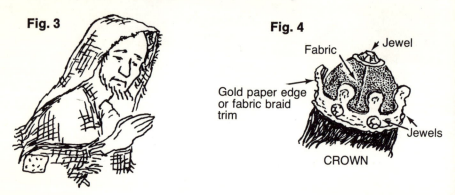

Most all edges should be covered with cord or braid to finish edge and avoid fraying. However, with poorer characters—peasant, shepherds, or a beggarman—the fraying can add to the character (Fig. 3). The kings should be lavished with elegant trims. Edge with gold braid, add fake fur. Trim with tiny beads and fake jewels (available at craft store). Use gold braid or gold paper edging for crowns (Fig. 4) and gifts.

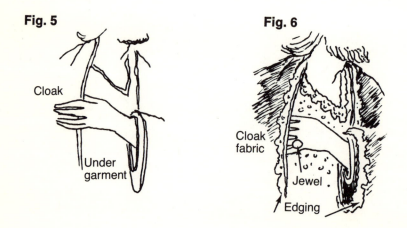

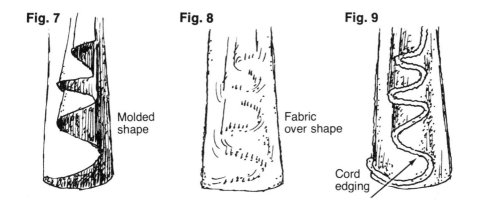

Fig. 7 Molded shape

Fig. 8 Fabric over shape

Fig. 9 Cord edging

The gestures of some figures may present a problem (Fig. 5); work trims around as needed (Fig. 6). A cloak may have self folds (Fig. 7) molded in. Cover area with one piece of fabric (Fig. 8). Reestablish contours with cord edging (Fig. 9).

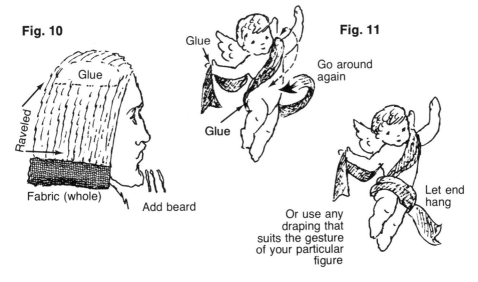

Fig. 10

Glue

Raveled

Fabric (whole)

Add beard

Glue

Glue

Fig. 11

Go around again

Let end hang

Or use any draping that suits the gesture of your particular figure

For hair, use unraveled yarn or fabric. A thin fabric often has a good kink when unraveled. To cover head, cut small piece; unravel almost to end of piece. Glue threads to top of head (Fig. 10). When dry, unravel remainder. Add glue beneath. Using wax paper under fingers, press on strands to create a hair-do. Cut small wisps for beards and glue on.

For cherubim, cut narrow strips of thin material and wind around bodies (Fig. 11). Glue in necessary spots to hold, leaving some ends hanging. Add hair as described, if desired.

These figures, molded of black plastic, often with inaccurately painted features, were found in the novelty section of Woolworths. By carefully repainting where needed and adding fabrics, they attained the classic look of antique presepio figurines. The shepherd with the horn has blue wool pants and a tunic of brown terrycloth. Raveled burlap type garments give the beggarman his character.

Assemble on background, placing figures in position. Add sheep, chickens, dogs—anything of appropriate size to give feeling of town life. If using a horse (see photo), add fabric and gold braid trappings and a fake hair mane. By now your own ingenuity will take over for figures and trim ideas to use.

The cherubim usually have a wire at the back. Poke the wire through the papiêr-maché. Place on columns (see photo) or above the central figures. Glue if needed. Select proper-sized star from tree trims or package decorations. Glue or wire in place.

Add branches, dried or artificial greenery, straw on ground, or whatever seems to enhance the mood. It's your creation. Children as well as adults enjoy this presepio. It's sturdy enough so children can rearrange it, an involvement so important to the holiday season.

Various techniques discussed in this book were used to create these tree ornaments. At left, macro-lace is plaited on a bracelet, a miniature mosaic was made in a shell. The triangular tree is suede leather. In the center, a Christmas card picture is enhanced with veneer; cut veneers create the angel. The three-sided dimensional ornament is made of shiny foil Christmas cards and the filigree decoration is quillwork.

Ornaments: In Review

The craft techniques described in this book can be creatively combined for your own needs and interests. A few suggestions follow, as a sort of summary of methods inspired by Italian crafts. Although Italians have only recently adopted the custom of decorating a Christmas tree, the crafts we've described adapt well to making trims. Holiday ornaments are fun to make, they sell well at Christmas bazaars, and because of their small size, they can use up leftover materials from larger projects. Handmade ornaments are always delightful around the holidays to give as gifts or to use for special package decorations.

There are other possible uses for a small decorative unit 3″ across. You can hang it on a chain for a pendant, or on a cord for a key ring or shade pull. Or you might assemble several for a mobile.

Here are some ideas and patterns to get you started on your own creations. I've made the following descriptions brief, assuming you are now familiar with each craft, so it might be wise to reread the instructions for the particular craft used. For instance: To make an overlay ornament, using veneer scraps, see the instructions for making bookends in Chapter 4.

Few new materials will be needed. It's assumed you'll have scraps. To give holiday sparkle, though, a spool of gold cord (available in craft stores) would be useful. Tinsel cord about 1/32″ thick is a thread wound with gold (or silver). As the gold tends to separate when used for sewing, it's better for gluing and braiding. Lamé cord, slightly thinner, can be used for sewing as well as other crafts. Either can be used for hangers. Or use transparent fishing line (about 6 pounds test weight) for hanging the ornaments. Loop through hole in top (Fig. 1) and tie as shown (Fig. 2). Also, save old Christmas cards; they are useful in all sorts of ways.

Tools and boards will not be listed under materials, assuming you already have these from working the original craft. Only the special materials needed for each ornament will be listed.

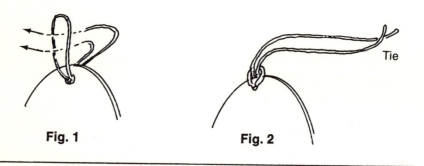

Fig. 1   **Fig. 2**

Bobbin Lace

Materials: narrow plastic or imitation gold bracelet (from dime store); gold tinsel cord; bobbins; cardboard; beads; pins.

Once you have learned the bobbin lace technique (see Chapter 1, Macro-Lace), it's possible to make lovely, lacy ornaments. Cut eight cords about 26″ long. Fold cords in half and mount on bracelet. Pin onto the cardboard. Plait the design, adding beads as you work. When near the middle, make braids on either side long enough to go out to edge (Fig. 1). Go around bracelet, work braid back toward center, and continue, making a woven area. Braid again near lower edge. Put one pair of the braid over, other pair under (Fig. 2), to attach to lower edge of bracelet. Continue braiding, add beads, continue about 1″ below bracelet. Tie and trim off (Fig. 3). Tie on hanging cord. Any combination of stitches is possible within this framework; try your own designs.

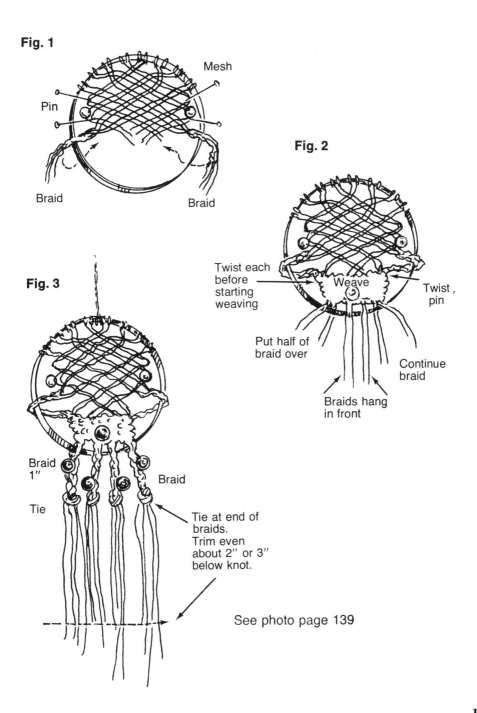

Fig. 1

Mesh

Pin

Braid

Braid

Fig. 2

Twist each before starting weaving

Weave

Twist, pin

Put half of braid over

Continue braid

Fig. 3

Braids hang in front

Braid 1″

Braid

Tie

Tie at end of braids. Trim even about 2″ or 3″ below knot.

See photo page 139

Shell Mosaic

Materials: shell; gold cord; dyed eggshells; gold angel figure about 1¼″ high (from craft store); iridescent and clear nail polish; glue.

Select (or purchase) a scallop shell about 2″ high (or any similar shell). Clean shell, and when dry, cover with thin coat of iridiscent nail polish. (For the one shown in photo, sparkle gold nail polish covers a worn shell back.)

Plan a design which will enhance basic shape of shell, not contradict it (Fig. 1). Add glue to inside of shell; glue in the gold cord to separate the areas (see Chapter 2, Mini-Mosaics). Add the eggshell mosaics. While gluing, attach hanging cord to top and add extra piece of eggshell to cover. When glue is dry, cover mosaic with clear nail polish. When dry, glue in angel or any other figure desired.

Any of the pendant designs for eggshell mosaics, when made in appropriate colors, could be used for ornaments. Glue design to cardboard or into shallow jar top; edge with gold foil or cord (Fig. 2).

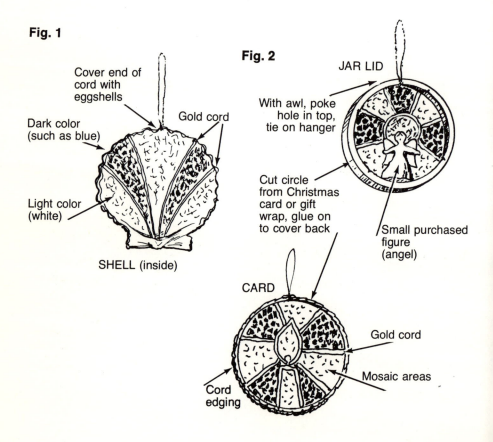

Fig. 1

Cover end of cord with eggshells

Gold cord

Dark color (such as blue)

Light color (white)

SHELL (inside)

Fig. 2

JAR LID

With awl, poke hole in top, tie on hanger

Cut circle from Christmas card or gift wrap, glue on to cover back

Small purchased figure (angel)

CARD

Gold cord

Mosaic areas

Cord edging

Leather

Materials: scraps from elbow patches (see Chapter 4, Petite Patch Pouch), or scraps of suede leather (from craft store); cardboard; gold lamé cord or gift wrap cord; gold soutache or other trim about ⅛″ wide; glue.

For tree, trace Fig. 1 on paper. Cut curved shapes of alternate light and dark suede, making slightly wider at each side. Trace tree outline and cut of medium-weight cardboard. Spread glue on card, position the largest suede piece, and add gold cord along edge. Position next suede piece, butting against gold cord. Repeat, placing gold cord between each cut edge. Press down firmly and allow to dry. Trim even with edges of card. Repeat for other side, or make one overall piece of suede on reverse side. Trim edges even. Glue gold soutache along outside edges. Glue hanger at top, under edging; continue gluing on edging.

Any traditional shape—bell, ball, wreath, etc.—could be made in this manner. For a key ring, make a triangle or circle; cover with suede design. Make a hole with awl in one edge; attach to key ring with a jump link (Fig. 2).

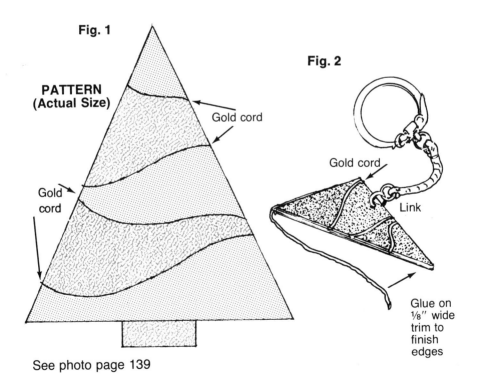

Fig. 1

**PATTERN
(Actual Size)**

Gold cord

Gold cord

See photo page 139

Fig. 2

Gold cord

Link

Glue on ⅛″ wide trim to finish edges

Wood

Materials: veneer scraps (or strips of veneer edging from hardware store); veneer borders, clear acrylic spray (or spray-on varnish or nail polish); depending on design—Christmas cards, paint, or seeds.

To frame a miniature of a famous artist's rendering of the nativity scene, select an appropriate picture from a Christmas card, about 3″ or 3½″

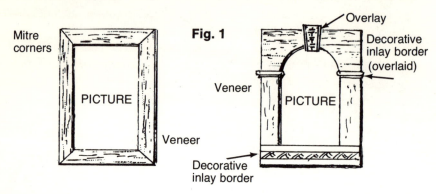

Fig. 1

Mitre corners

PICTURE

Veneer

Decorative inlay border

Overlay

Decorative inlay border (overlaid)

Veneer

PICTURE

high. Plan wood to enhance scene (Fig. 1). For square framing, corners should be mitered. Include some decorative inlay borders, if you have some left over. Ornament should not be much more than 5″ high to hang on tree. However, for wall hangings or other uses, any size could be made.

Fig. 2

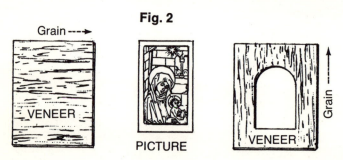

Grain ---→

VENEER

PICTURE

Grain ----→

VENEER

Cut wood (see Chapter 4, Overlay: Bird Bookends). Cut a backing of veneer, making grain go in opposite directions (Fig. 2). Glue picture to backing; gluc frame over. Sand edges even, if necessary. Add decorations. A hanger cord can be glued between layers, or, after ornament is completed, make a hole with awl in center top. Tie on a cord. If a thicker, more substantial decoration is desired, use ⅛″ balsa to make a core (see Chapter 4, Balsa Core Jewelry).

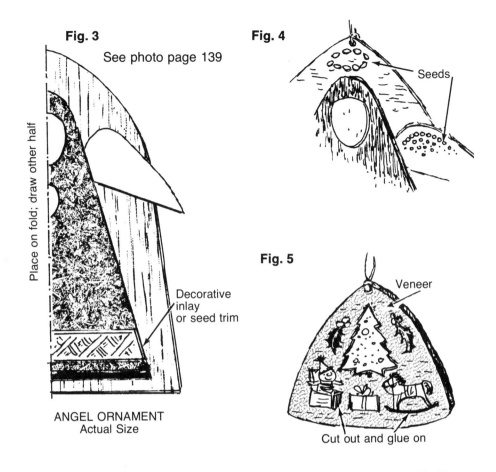

Fig. 3

See photo page 139

Place on fold; draw other half

Fig. 4

Seeds

Fig. 5

Veneer

Decorative
inlay
or seed trim

ANGEL ORNAMENT
Actual Size

Cut out and glue on

For an angel design, trace Fig. 3 on paper; draw other half. For background, trace outline on veneer. Cut two, with grain in opposite directions. Glue together, sand edges. Trace outline of wings, face, and hands on light veneer, body on a dark veneer. Cut out. Glue in position. Add seed decorations as desired. Hold seed with tweezers, dip in glue, and set in position. Halo and skirt trim could be sesame seed; mustard seed trims for wings (Fig. 4). Spray varnish; add hanger. If you don't have any veneers, attractive but not as durable ornaments could be made of colored cardboard, layered in this manner with seeds added.

Veneer (with balsa core or just two veneer layers) can also make good backgrounds for decoupage (see Chapter 5, Art Povero). Select several small motifs from a Christmas card or gift wrap paper. If using a card, peel off back layers, making picture area as thin as possible. Cut carefully and place units on the wood (Fig. 5). Glue in position. Cover with clear nail polish.

Card Construction

Materials: old Christmas cards; embroidery floss or lamé cord; needle.

The method of attaching cards to each other (see Chapter 5, Card Creations) can be used to make dimensional decorations. Trace shape (Fig. 1) on lightweight paper. Lay over Christmas cards to find proper-size designs to make ornament. You may find similar colors and designs to use from several cards or possibly find a card with repeated motifs (Fig. 2) in a position so three could be cut of one card. Shape could be changed slightly, if necessary, to fit card design.

Using pattern, cut three units, and buttonhole-stitch around the edge of each with embroidery floss. Attach together, leaving 2″ or more hanging top and bottom. Tie top for a hanger. Tie in another extra length of embroidery floss at bottom (Fig. 3) to form a tassel.

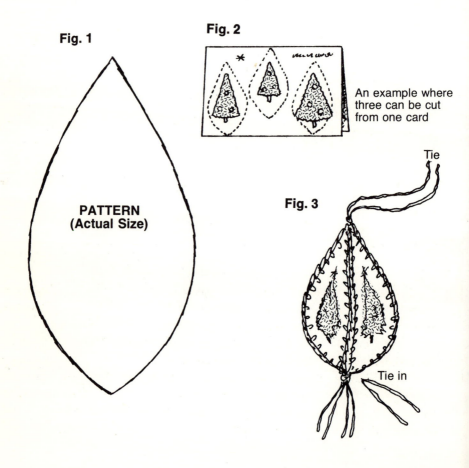

Fig. 1

Fig. 2

An example where three can be cut from one card

PATTERN (Actual Size)

Fig. 3

Tie

Tie in

Quillwork

Materials: strips of quilling paper; bone or gold curtain rings (1″ or less diameter); jewels or beads; glue.

Make delicate ornaments entirely of quilling (see Chapter 5, Paper Filigree), or add some reinforcement, which also adds dimension to the design.

On folded paper, trace design A (Fig. 1); trace other half, open up, and place under the wax paper on the quilling board. Quill the shapes indicated. Trace and quill shape B (Fig. 2). When glue is set, lift off wax paper. Glue curtain ring to quilling A, and glue design B on top of ring.

Glue fake jewels or beads into round coils in the design, as desired. Use transparent fishing line for hanging cord; tie to ring, then tie up through top coil. Try various combinations of quilled shapes; they create a lacy snowflake look. Try making a wreath of pinched coils using a plastic bracelet as the reinforcement.

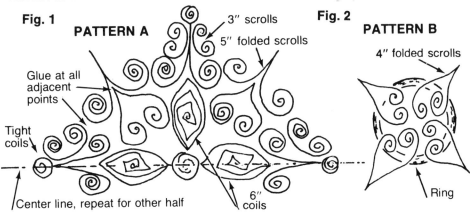

Fig. 1

PATTERN A

3″ scrolls

5″ folded scrolls

Glue at all adjacent points

Tight coils

Center line, repeat for other half

6″ coils

Fig. 2

PATTERN B

4″ folded scrolls

Ring

rnaments, holiday trims—the possibilities are endless. There are enough crafts in this book to make all kinds. Try a mosaic of various materials, such as cut up cards, to create designs; or tambour a circle, or inlay a trinket into balsa. Paint designs on wood veneer. Or chip carve balsa and paint it bright, cheerful colors. Straw work is a natural for Christmas.

The preceding directions and patterns were just to get you started. After making a craft once, creating on your own is easier. Italian crafts have been discussed here for inspiration, not imitation. Let's hope these techniques and designs will spark your own creativity.

7

GENERAL
INFORMATION

Materials:

Most of the projects in this book adapted or simplified classic methods in order to utilize easily available materials from local stores or use up scraps and discards found around the house. Save the rigid foam corners that are used for packing fragile objects, save old Christmas cards, cardboard from pad backs and old gift boxes. Hoard old jewelry, collect scraps of fabrics. Many may be useful for various projects. For patterns, use onionskin, old dress patterns, or tracing paper, available at art supply stores. For specialized craft materials, a list of suppliers is included in this chapter.

Basic Tools:

For most crafts, pencil, paper, ruler, scissors, a knife, such as an X-acto (see chart Fig. 1), white glue, and masking tape should be kept handy. Most are easily available. Clamps such as stationery clips, clip clothespins, or weights are often needed when gluing. Spread old newspapers or use a piece of cardboard to protect working surfaces. Use all tools carefully, taking any precautions necessary, keeping safety in mind.

Fig. 1

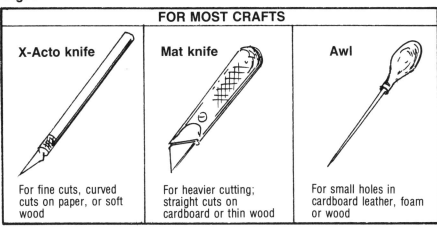

FOR MOST CRAFTS

X-Acto knife

For fine cuts, curved cuts on paper, or soft wood

Mat knife

For heavier cutting; straight cuts on cardboard or thin wood

Awl

For small holes in cardboard leather, foam or wood

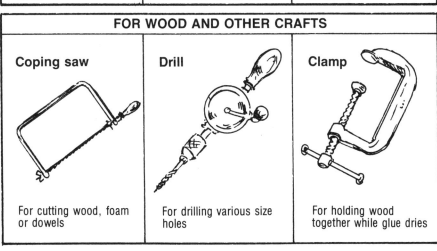

FOR WOOD AND OTHER CRAFTS

Coping saw

For cutting wood, foam or dowels

Drill

For drilling various size holes

Clamp

For holding wood together while glue dries

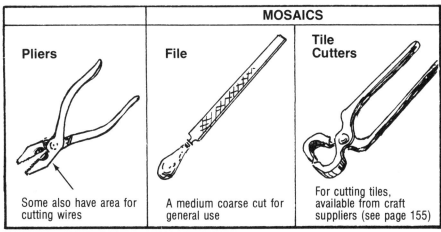

MOSAICS

Pliers

Some also have area for cutting wires

File

A medium coarse cut for general use

Tile Cutters

For cutting tiles, available from craft suppliers (see page 155)

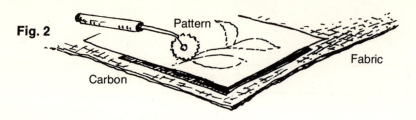

Fig. 2

Pattern

Fabric

Carbon

Stitchery:

For most projects, keep on hand needle, thread, pins, and thimble. Also, you may need embroidery floss, embroidery hoop, crochet cotton, or yarn. All are available at local department, dime, or sewing stores.

To transfer a pattern onto fabric, use a dressmaker's carbon and wheel (Fig. 2). Place fabric on firm surface, lay carbon over, with pattern on top. Run wheel over lines on pattern.

Most sewing can be done by hand; however machine sewing makes a more even and secure seam in less time. If possible, use a sewing machine when suggested.

A few basic embroidery stitches are shown (Fig. 3). The basic stitch for needle lace is the buttonhole stitch (and its many variations).

Fig. 3

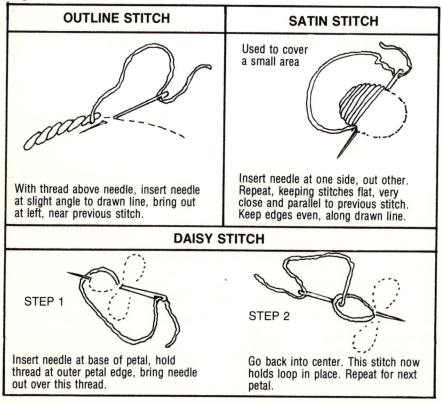

OUTLINE STITCH	SATIN STITCH
With thread above needle, insert needle at slight angle to drawn line, bring out at left, near previous stitch.	Used to cover a small area. Insert needle at one side, out other. Repeat, keeping stitches flat, very close and parallel to previous stitch. Keep edges even, along drawn line.

DAISY STITCH

STEP 1
Insert needle at base of petal, hold thread at outer petal edge, bring needle out over this thread.

STEP 2
Go back into center. This stitch now holds loop in place. Repeat for next petal.

Fig. 3 Continued

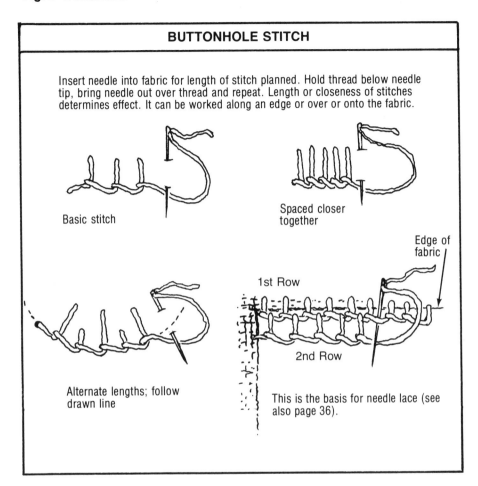

BUTTONHOLE STITCH

Insert needle into fabric for length of stitch planned. Hold thread below needle tip, bring needle out over thread and repeat. Length or closeness of stitches determines effect. It can be worked along an edge or over or onto the fabric.

Basic stitch

Spaced closer together

Edge of fabric

1st Row

2nd Row

Alternate lengths; follow drawn line

This is the basis for needle lace (see also page 36).

Wood:

Special tools for wood (see chart Fig. 1) include a coping saw, awl, knife, sandpaper, clamps, and possibly a file or drill. All are available at variety and hardware stores. To transfer a pattern to a hard surface, blacken the back of the pattern with a soft pencil. Tape pattern in place on surface. Go over lines with a sharp pencil and then remove pattern.

Paints:

Acrylic paints are usually suggested for all surfaces, since they thin with water but dry permanently. Some variety stores carry these paints, as do all art and craft stores.

Glues:

Many kinds of glues are available; check with your hardware store or craft store for special ones, and follow instructions on label. White glue (Elmer's, Ad-a-Grip) serves most purposes. Sobo will hold on Stryofoam and fabrics as well as paper and wood. Use household cement (Duco) for metallic or other nonporous surfaces. New products constantly become available; check with your local hardware store about any special glues for the material you are using.

Finishes:

To preserve and finish, often a clear acrylic spray is recommended. Art and craft stores carry a variety of these sprays, such as Krylon, Blair Fixitive, and Tuffilm. For wood, there are spray-on varnishes and acrylic coatings as well as the brush-on varieties.

Jewelry Findings:

There are many jewelry findings available (see chart Fig. 4), some locally, others from craft suppliers. With a little practice, it's possible to assemble all types of jewelry. Use small-nosed pliers to twist links and eye pins. To open a link (Fig. 5), twist it sideways slightly (do not open out). Slip opened ring into chain or next link and twist closed. This avoids ruining the circular shape. To make a chain desired length, open links as needed.

To assemble beads with eye pins (Fig. 6), slide a bead on a pin and roll straight end around tip of pliers, forming a round loop at other side of bead. Link bead units together (Fig. 7).

Bell caps, bails, and up-eyes (Fig. 8) are glued to top of a decorative unit to provide hole for linking to chain or cord. A small piece holds with household cement. Use clear epoxy for larger units. This glue comes in two tubes—equal amounts of each to be mixed. Follow instructions on package. For instance, glue a bell cap to a pretty shell, and link onto a thin thong.

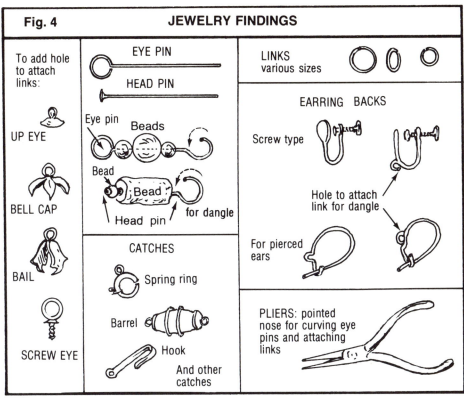

Fig. 4 — JEWELRY FINDINGS

To add hole to attach links:

UP EYE

BELL CAP

BAIL

SCREW EYE

EYE PIN

HEAD PIN

Eye pin
Beads

Bead
Bead
for dangle
Head pin

CATCHES

Spring ring

Barrel

Hook

And other catches

LINKS various sizes

EARRING BACKS

Screw type

Hole to attach link for dangle

For pierced ears

PLIERS: pointed nose for curving eye pins and attaching links

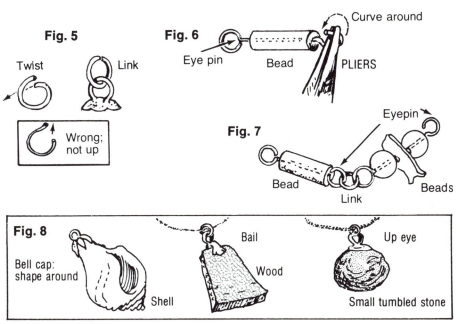

Fig. 5

Twist

Link

Wrong; not up

Fig. 6

Eye pin   Bead   PLIERS

Curve around

Fig. 7

Eyepin

Bead

Link

Beads

Fig. 8

Bell cap: shape around

Shell

Bail

Wood

Up eye

Small tumbled stone

To Enlarge Patterns:

Make a ½″ grid on thin paper. Lay paper over design in book and trace pattern. On a larger piece of paper, draw a grid of 1″ squares (unless otherwise indicated). Now draw outline on the larger grid (Fig. 9) using small one as a guide, and counting corresponding squares as necessary. This enables you to establish proper proportions on the larger drawing.

Fig. 9

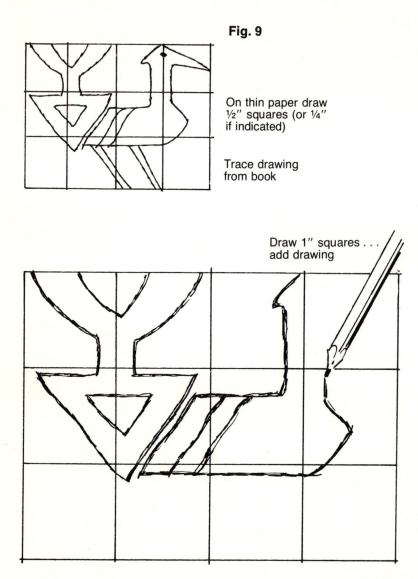

On thin paper draw
½″ squares (or ¼″
if indicated)

Trace drawing
from book

Draw 1″ squares . . .
add drawing

Craft Materials Suppliers

With the increased interest in crafts today, many materials needed can be found at local department, hardware, or variety stores. Many such stores now carry some craft materials and some jewelry findings. Most stitchery materials can be found locally in specialty shops or sewing sections of larger stores. Selecting texture and color combinations is easier when they can be seen and compared.

Specialized craft materials are available at local art and craft stores. American Handicrafts (Tandy Crafts, Inc.) has stores in most all major cities (check in the phone book). They carry a wide variety of materials.

There are also many mail-order craft suppliers. Some, such as the two below, carry a full line of all kinds of materials: boxes, plaques, decoupage materials, jewelry supplies, quilling paper strips, gold cord, beads, leather, shells, and so on.

> FLORIDA SUPPLY HOUSE, P.O. Box 847, Brandenton, Fla. 33507. (Inquire about catalog.)

> LEE WARDS, Dept. 9116, 1200 St. Charles St., Elgin, Ill. 60120. (Request a free catalog.)

Other suppliers specialize. Since catalog costs change, it is best to write and inquire about price (if any) of the catalog, or request information about the specific item wanted.

Lace:
> Lace making tools, booklets, and patterns:
> SOME PLACE, 2990 Adeline St., Berkeley, Cal. 94703.

Mosaics:
> Tiles (as well as many other craft materials for schools and groups):
> S & S ARTS AND CRAFTS, Colchester, Conn. 16415.

Wood:
> Veneers, decorative inlays, and borders:
> ALBERT CONSTANTINE AND SON, INC., 2050 Eastchester Rd., Bronx, N.Y. 10461.

Straw:
> PAUL STRAIGHT CRAFT SUPPLIES, Yarrow, Mo. 63501. (No catalog.)

Decoupage:
Most craft stores carry these supplies. For prints: DOVER PUBLICA-
TIONS, INC. At local book dealers or write Dept. DA, 180 Varick St.,
New York, N.Y. 10014. (Request catalog on decoupage print books.)

Jewelry supplies:
SY SCHWEITZER & CO. INC., P.O. Box 60999, Sunnyvale, Cal. 94088

Bibliography

Some books give background and history for an individual craft, others
discuss methods with instructions for actual projects. Some cover both.
There are many books on each topic, but only space here for a few. New
books come out each year. If further information is needed on a subject that
especially interests you, look in the library index or on the shelf for adjacent
books. Some of the books listed below have extensive bibliographies on
their specific topics. Only English language sources are listed here.

General:
Bossert, Helmut Theodor. *Folk Art of Europe*. New York: Praeger, 1953.
Vaussard, Maurice. *Daily Life in 18th Century Italy*. New York: Macmil-
lan, 1963.

Chapter 1: With a bit of Thread
Bath, Virginia. *Lace*. Chicago: Henry Regnery, 1974.
Christenson, Jo Ippolito. *Trapunto*. New York: Sterling, 1972.
Guild, Vera. *New Complete Book of Needlecraft*. New York: Good House-
keeping Books, 1971.
Katzenberg, Gloria. *Art and Stitchery*. New York: Scribner, 1974.
Kliot, Kaethe and Jules. *Bobbin Lace*. New York: Crown, 1973.
Marein, Shirley. *Stitchery, Needlepoint, Applique and Patchwork*. New
York: Viking, 1974.
Nordfors, Jill. *Needle Lace and Needle Weaving*. New York: Van Nos-
trand Reinhold, 1974.
Wooster, A. *Quiltmaking, The Modern Approach to an Old Craft*. New
York: Drake, 1972.

Chapter 2: Mosaics

Arvois, Edmond. *Making Mosaics*. New York: Sterling, 1964.

Hutton, Helen. *Mosaic Making*. New York: Van Nostrand Reinhold, 1966.

Stribling, Mary Lou. *Mosaic Techniques*. New York: Crown, 1966.

Chapter 3: Leather

Newman, Thelma. *Leather as an Art and Craft*. New York: Crown, 1973.

Waterer, John William. *Leather Craftsmanship*. New York: Praeger, 1968.

Wilcox and Manning. *Leather*. Chicago: Henry Regnery, 1972.

Chapter 4: Wood and Straw

Campkin, Marie. *Introducing Marquetry*. New York: Drake, 1970.

Hoppe, H. *Whittling and Wood Carving*. New York: Sterling, 1974.

Meilach, Donna. *Contemporary Art with Wood*. New York: Crown, 1968.

Chapter 5: Paper

D'Amato, Janet. *Quillwork, the Art of Paper Filigree*. New York: Evans, 1975.

Manning, Hiram. *Manning on Decoupage*. Great Neck, N.Y.: Hearthside, 1969.

Newman, Thelma. *Paper as an Art and Craft*. New York: Crown, 1973.

————*Contemporary Decoupage*. New York: Crown, 1972.

Chapter 6: Combined Materials, Toys and Celebrations

Baird, Bil. *The Art of the Puppet*. New York: Ridge, 1973.

De Robeck, Nesta. *The Christmas Crib*. Milwaukee: Bruce, 1956.

Raggio, Olga. *The Nativity, the Christmas Creche at the Metropolitan Museum of Art*. New York: Doubleday, 1965.

INDEX

Accessories
  petite patch pouch, 71-75
  see also jewelry
Apron, embroidered, 18-21
Ariosto, 116
Art Povero, 104-107

Balsa jewelry, 91-95
Bobbin lace, history of, 15-16
  sampler, 39-48
  ornament, 140-141
Book-ends, overlay, 85-87
Books, history of, 101-102
Bottles, leather covered, 68, 69-70
Boxes
  straw covered, 96-98
  fabric covered, 21-24
  decoupage, 105-107
  veneered, 88-90
Bracelet, 95
Buratto, 13

Card Christmas ornaments, 146
Candle and base, 80-84
Carving, 76-77
  chip, 80-84
Catholic Church, 12, 63, 77
  influence on Italian art, 9
Chinoiserie, 103-104
Clothes
  embroidered apron, 18-21
Christmas
  cards, 108-110, 144, 145, 146
  celebrations, 118
  manger scene 118, *see* Presepio
  tree ornaments, 139-147
Crocheting, 15
  stitch in Tambour, 29
Cutwork, 13

de Brecia, Muzio, 49
Decoupage, *see* Art Povero

Earrings, 153
  balsa core, 94-95
Embossing, of leather, 63
Embroidery, 13
  apron, 18-25
  basic stitches of, 150-151
  with trapunto, 28
  Punto in aria, 33-38

Epiphany, 118
Etruscan crafts, 9
Etruscan mosaics, 49

Festivals, 117-118
Figurines, presepio, 134-138
Filigree, paper, 104, 111-114
Florentine trapunto, 25-28
Folk art and crafts, 9-10
  chip carving as, 80
  leather in, 63
  mosaics in, 51-52
Folk dress, 17

Glues, 152
Gold, in lace, 12
Greeting cards
  creations with, 59, 105, 108-111,
    144
  history of, 104
Gutenberg, 102

Inlay, history of, 77
Intarsia, 77
Italy
  art of, 9
  folk art of, 9-10

Jewelry
  Balsa core, 91-95
  earrings, 94-95
  findings for, 152
  mini-mosaic, 59-61
  necklace, 91-94
  potshard pendants, 58

Key ring, 143
Knitting, 14
Knotting, *see* macrame

Lacche Povero, 104
Lace, 12
  bobbin lace, 15-16
  book of, 102
  macro-lace, 39-48
  needle laces, 14, sampler 33-38
Lacquerware, art of, 103-104
Leather, techniques of, 63
Leather crafts, 62-75
  bank, 64-68
  encased bottles, 69-70

ornament, 143
patch pouch, 71-75
Leather guilds, 63

Macrame, 15.
Macro-lace, 39-48
   as ornament, 140-141
Marionettes
   history of, 115-116
   Orlando, 116-117
   Pinocchio Puppet, 122-127
Marquetry, 79
Materials, 148-156
   collecting, 148
   glues, 152
   jewelry findings, 152-153
   paints, 152
   supply sources, 155-156
Midden mosaics, 54-57
Miniatures, mosaic, 51
Mini-mosaics, 59-61
Mosaics, as religious decorations, 49
Mosaics, methods, 52-53
Mosaic arts, history of, 49-53
Mosaic crafts, 49-61
   midden mosaics, 54-57
   mini mosaics, 59-61
   potshard pendants, 58
   shell mosaic ornament, 142
   Tesserae, 49

Necklace, balsa core, 91-94
Needle lace, 14-15.
   sampler, 33-36
   mirror frame, 36-38
Needlework
   punto tirato, buratto, 13
   see also Embroidery, Thread
      Crafts, Needle lace
Netting, 15

"Orlando Furioso," 116-117
Ornaments, 139-147
   Bobbin lace ornament, 140-141
   card construction, 146
   leather, 143
   paper quillwork, 147
   shell mosaic, 142
   wood, 144-145
Overlay, book-ends, 85-87

Paints, 152
Paper, development of, 101
Paper Crafts, 101-114
   card creations, 108-111
   card ornaments, 146
   filigree, 111-114
   quick trick art povero, 105-107
   quillwork, 147
Papier Maché, use in presepio, 133
Parquetry, 79
Patterns, enlargement of, 154
Pendants
   potshard, 58
   mini mosaic, 59-61
   wood, 91-95, 139
Pillow, trapunto, 25
Pot holder, 31
Plaque, straw, 99-100
Potshard pendants, 58
Pouch, leather, 71-75
Presepio
   construction of, 129-138
   history of, 118-121
Printing, development of, 102-104
Punch and Judy, 116
Punto in aria, 14, 33-38
Punto tagliato, 13
Punto tirato, 13
Puppets, *see* Marionettes

Quilting, 12
Quillwork (paper filigree), 104
   crafts, 111-114, 147

Renaissance, 9
   lace in, 12
   leather in, 63
   marquetry in, 79
   mosaics in, 50
Renaissance jewel box, 21-24
Reticella lace, 14
Rocco, Gregorio, 121
Rodia, Simon, 51-52
Roman crafts, 9
Rome
   leather use in, 62-63
   mosaics of, 49

Sconce, 54
Silver, in lace, 12
Stitchery techniques, 150-151

Straw, marquetry, 79
Straw crafts, 96-100
    marquetry box, 96-98
    plaque, 99-100
Supply sources, 155-156

Tambour, 28-32
Tesserae, 49, 52-53
Thread crafts, 11-48
    Bobbin lace, 15-16
    Bobbin lace ornament, 140-141
    Embroidery, 12
    Apron, 18-21
    Florentine trapunto, 25-28
    Folk dress, 17
    lace, 12
    Macro-lace, 39-48
    needle laces, 14
    punto in aria, 33-38
    punto tirato, 13
    quilting, 12
    Renaissance jewel box, 21-24
    Tambour, 28-32
    Trapunto, 12
Tools, 148, 149
Toys, 9, 76, 115
Trapunto, 12, 25, 28

Tray, 56, 88
Trivet, 55
Tote bag, 31-32
Turtle bank, 64-68

Vatican, 50
Veneer
    inlay technique, 88-90
    jewelry, 91-95
    ornaments, 144-145
    overlay book-ends, 85-87

Watts Tower, 52
Wood, tools for, 151
Wood crafts, 76-95
    balsa jewelry, 91-95
    chip carving, 80-84
    inlay veneer, 88-90
    ornaments, 144-145
    overlay book-ends, 85-87
    Pinocchio, puppet, 122-127

Yarn, used in
    Needlelace, 33-36
    Tambour, 29-32
    Trapunto, 25-28
    with leather, 71-75

PICTURE CREDITS

The METROPOLITAN MUSEUM OF ART, Rogers Fund, 1920, page 13.
The METROPOLITAN MUSEUM OF ART, The Mabel Metcalf Fahnestock Collection, Gift of Ruth Fahnestock Schermerhorn and Faith Fahnestock, 1933, page 14.
The METROPOLITAN MUSEUM OF ART, Gift of Mrs. Magdelena Nuttall, 1908, page 15.
The METROPOLITAN MUSEUM OF ART, Gift of George Blumenthal, 1941, page 76.
The METROPOLITAN MUSEUM OF ART, Rogers Fund, 1913, page 77.
The METROPOLITAN MUSEUM OF ART, Rogers Fund, 1939, page 78.
The METROPOLITAN MUSEUM OF ART, Fletcher Fund, 1925, page 103.
"ENIT," ITALIAN GOVERNMENT TRAVEL OFFICE, pages 16, 50, 52, 53, 117, 118, 119, 120.
DOVER PUBLICATIONS reprint of *Renaissance Patterns for Lace, Embroidery and Needlepoint,* pages 1, 12, 102.
"ENIT," ROMA, courtesy of ITALIAN CULTURAL INSTITUTE, pages 11, 17.
N.Y. PUBLIC LIBRARY, picture collection, page 116 top, page 101.
Puppet from the THOMA collection, page 116.